I Can't Believe I Dated Him

In this day and age women don't really need men. We have our own careers, we can wield a hammer, and join self-protection classes to take care of ourselves but many women still want companionship and the connection of deep intimacy with one special man. The dating and searching for this special soulmate has been fraught with all sorts of problems because of our stinkin' thinkin' conditioning by our parents, our culture, and the times we live in. In *I Can't Believe I Dated Him*, author Jackie Viramontez expertly and compassionately guides you to do more inner searching for emotional patterns and behaviours so that the wrong men stop appearing at your doorsteps. I highly recommend this book for single or married women looking for a step- by- step approach to turn relationship pains into opportunities for self-discovery and a chance for lasting joy.

—**Alina Frank**, EFT Tapping Trainer and
Bestselling Author of *How to Want Sex Again*

Jackie Viramontez brilliantly shares her wisdom, wit and science to provide you with practical solutions that will propel you into the relationship you deserve with a special partner, and with yourself! The simple process teaches you to use your emotions as a guidance system to transform your relationships in hours rather than decades, or a lifetime. Women of every stage of life need to read *I Can't Believe I Dated Him!*

—**Dale Paula Teplitz**, M.A., EFT Tapping Expert,
Trainer and Mentor

Brilliant! Jackie is spot on in *I Can't Believe I Dated Him*! Relationships whether pre or post marriage are all about what we learned emotionally earlier in life. Emotional Freedom Techniques (EFT "tapping") are the tool to undo all those hard-wired, neurochemical lessons, allowing us to move forward to become who we are meant to be and to find that soul-mate God has waiting for us.

How do I know this? God, using the techniques laid out in this book, saved our marriage. Six years ago, before learning Emotional Freedom Techniques, my marriage was dead; divorce was imminent. No amount of counseling worked. We wanted the relationship saved, but it was doomed. We fought daily. Later, after learning EFT, we realized our marriage wasn't about either of us; it was about relational childhood lessons we needed to upgrade.

EFT is the great eraser. Learn to "tap", release the underlying emotions pinning you to habits that don't support dating and marriage, and watch both of you grow, learning to live and love beyond anything you ever imagined!

—**Sherrie Rice Smith, R.N.**, Author of EFT for Christians,
EFT Trainer and Instructor

Beautiful, reassuring, and vulnerable, *I Can't Believe I Dated Him* unfolds with the deeper truth of what it means to be in relationship: discovering ourselves through the mirror of others and having the courage to approach what we learn as an opportunity for transformation. This amazing book should be required reading for everyone: single, dating, or married."

—**Sue Rasmussen**, Bestselling Author of
My Desk Is Driving Me Crazy and Life Coach

Whether you are in a relationship or not, this book is an absolute must read. Reading this transformed my taken-for-granted ideas about emotions like anxiety, insecurity and anger. Instead of "getting rid of" negative emotions, this book inspires eye-opening, if not life-changing, revelations about what emotions really are. This is the first book I've seen that objectively brings to light the fact that emotions (like any other brain signal) have an evolutionary purpose. By taking a step back to view emotions objectively for the first time, this book opens up a whole new way of experiencing every human thought and interaction. As an educator, I would also strongly recommend this book to adolescents and anyone who works with kids. Even the most "well-adjusted," respected, successful people unquestioningly accept that emotions affect behavior. This book lays out a simple step-by-step plan to erase that reality. For anyone in a relationship with a boyfriend, friend, coworker or boss, I do not know a single person who would not enjoy their life (and themselves) more after reading this book.

—**Lauren Martin, M.D.** Educator and Non Profit Founder

When I started reading *I Can't Believe I Dated Him*, I thought it must be some sort of prank and someone had obviously unearthed my dating life to build each chapter. It was a relief to be wrong and to know that I'm not alone in this journey. The powerful insight in these pages undid me and put me back together in a way I've needed for a long time. I've carried a lot of shame about my choices in men, but this book helped to acknowledge, heal, and transform the root of it all.

—**Danielle Bennett, M.D.** Poet, Communicator and Educator

Jackie's book addresses the trifecta of relationship mastery: Empowerment, Emotions, and Energy. Through clear explanations about negative emotions that arise from old belief systems, women who feel trapped in old patterns can begin to see a light at the end of a despairing tunnel. But Jackie doesn't just stop raising conscious awareness, she also provides the energy tools for transforming those old patterns into new relationship potentials. It's empowering to know that I can let go of what doesn't serve me now and anything that might come up in the future. No more holding back or failing in relationships!

—**Gia Combs-Ramirez**, Author of *The Way of Transformation: Discovering the Divine Map to Unlock your Highest Potential and Transformational Healer at New Science of Energy Healing*

I Can't Believe
I Dated
Him

THE ART OF KNOWING WHEN TO BREAK UP,
WHEN TO STAY SINGLE & WHEN YOU'VE MET

THE ONE

Jackie Viramontez

NEW YORK

NASHVILLE • MELBOURNE • VANCOUVER

I Can't Believe I Dated Him
The Art Of Knowing When To Break Up,
When To Stay Single & When You've Met THE ONE

Published in New York, New York, by Morgan James Publishing in partnership with Difference Press. Morgan James and The Entrepreneurial Publisher are trademarks of Morgan James, LLC. www.MorganJamesPublishing.com

The Morgan James Speakers Group can bring authors to your live event. For more information or to book an event visit The Morgan James Speakers Group at www.TheMorganJamesSpeakersGroup.com.

Shelfie

A free eBook edition is available with the purchase of this print book.

CLEARLY PRINT YOUR NAME ABOVE IN UPPER CASE

Instructions to claim your free eBook edition:
1. Download the Shelfie app for Android or iOS
2. Write your name in **UPPER CASE** above
3. Use the Shelfie app to submit a photo
4. Download your eBook to any device

ISBN 978-1-68350-280-7 paperback
ISBN 978-1-68350-281-4 eBook
ISBN 978-1-68350-282-1 hardcover
Library of Congress Control Number:
2016916535

Interior Design: Bonnie Bushman

Cover Design: Heidi Miller

Editing: Cynthia Kane

Author's photo courtesy of
Jake Viramontez

In an effort to support local communities, raise awareness and funds, Morgan James Publishing donates a percentage of all book sales for the life of each book to Habitat for Humanity Peninsula and Greater Williamsburg.

Get involved today! Visit
www.MorganJamesBuilds.com

Disclaimer

Please read the following before proceeding further.

The information presented in this book, title *I Can't Believe I Dated Him*, including ideas, suggestions, exercises, techniques, and other materials, is educational in nature and is provided only as general information. This book is solely intended for the reader's own self-improvement and is not meant to substitute medical or psychological treatment and does not replace services of health care professionals.

This book contains information regarding Emotional Freedom Techniques or EFT. EFT looks at and seeks to address stressors and imbalances within a person's energy system, as well as the energetic influence of thoughts, beliefs, and emotions in the body. EFT is based on ancient Chinese acupuncture that balances an individual's energy with a gentle tapping procedure. Tapping stimulates pressure points on the face and body while focusing on issues of emotional intensity in order to release the intensity and reframe the issues. The prevailing premise of EFT is that the flow and balance of the body's electromagnetic and more subtle energies are important for physical, spiritual, and emotional health, and for fostering well-being.

Although EFT appears to have promising emotional, spiritual, and physical health benefits, and there is a growing body of scientific research indicating that EFT is an effective evidence based technique, especially for managing stress, EFT has yet to be fully researched by the Western academic, medical, and psychological communities. Therefore, EFT may be considered experimental. The reader agrees to assume and accept full responsibility for any and all risks associated with reading this book and using EFT. If the reader inadvertently experiences any emotional distress or physical discomfort using EFT, the reader is advised to stop and to seek professional care, if appropriate.

Publishing of this information contained in this book is not intended to create a client-practitioner or any other type of professional relationship between the reader and the author. While the author is an experienced EFT practitioner and Reiki Master, the author is not a licensed health care provider. The author does not make any warranty, guarantee, or prediction regarding the outcome of an individual using EFT for any particular purpose or issue.

By continuing to read this book, the reader agrees to forever, fully release, indemnify, and hold harmless, the author, and others associated with the publication of this book from any claim or liability and for any damage or injury whatsoever kind or nature that the reader may incur arising at any time out of, or in relation to, the reader's use of the information presented in this book. If any court of law rules that any part of the disclaimer is invalid, the disclaimer stands as if those parts were struck out.

By continuing to read this book you agree to all of the above.

Dedication

To Lauren, for being proof that even the scariest of emotions will never overpower love.

And Jake, for redefining love every single day.

Table of Contents

PART ONE

Should My Relationship Be This Difficult?

"Consider it pure joy, my brothers and sisters,
whenever you face trials of many kinds."
—**James**, son of Alphaeus

1

Relationships Are Like Computers

♥ ♥ ♥

Feelings are opportunities to rebel against the voices that tell us
we are destined for less, so we can upgrade into our truth.

I couldn't believe it was happening again. I had spent five months in the dark, reading clues that something in his personality had changed. When I finally asked him, "Did you ever cheat on me while I was gone?" his hesitation gave him away.

"It's funny that you never asked me that until now."

Funny is not the adjective I would have chosen.

Four hours later he must have found his cajones in a drawer and mustered the courage to walk them over to my place and tell me what I already knew to be true. He had cheated on me. While I was studying abroad he let a few too many drinks and his sloppy dance moves lure one of my classmates into his bed.

Relationships. We crave them from our first Disney movie and detest them from our first heartbreak. We date winners, losers, winners who look like losers, and losers who convince us they are winners. No matter what we learn from relationship to relationship, we seem to bring the patterns with us, unfolding as the same issues in different contexts, and with different men. This was not my first boyfriend to cheat and lie. There had been three others who had convinced me to trust them, only to prove my initial intuition correct as I caught them red-handed in their pool of deceit. For years I thought there was something wrong with me, ashamed that I could be so naive, as if they could see gullible written on my forehead. Did my psyche have a sadistic love affair with feeling betrayed and manipulated? Or, did I just have poor taste in men?

Years later, happily married to a man who only uses manipulation to coax me out of a funk, I have a different theory. I've worked with hundreds of women and I have seen the same themes within their relationships.

Problems Are For You, Not Against You

Women are taught that relationship problems are patterns they should avoid. The theory that problems are inherently "negative" is harmful in two ways. First, this attitude teaches you to blame yourself when relationship difficulties strike. Secondly, it robs you of the higher purpose waiting within your issues. My theory is that relationship problems, like betrayal, heartbreak, and jealousy, repeat themselves for a different reason.

"Negative" relationships patterns don't show up to blame you, shame you, or punish you. What if you assumed that God, or whatever higher power you acknowledge, doesn't send problems your way so you will "fix" yourself. What if you assumed that your higher power is more interested in loving you then fixing you. Then, you can assume that problems exist to bring you into more wholeness, not more striving and self-editing.

Like an allergic reaction, the external rash is not necessarily the problem. The rash is a signal to deal with a bigger internal issue. In the same way, relationship problems are not so much a problem as a signal to deal with more important internal matters. Your current relationship problem is not happening to you, but for you. It is a signal, a signal that will bring you into more health and wholeness if you listen to it.

When I found out my boyfriend was cheating on me, I was not being punished for poor choice in men. I was not being called to "fix" anything about myself. I was getting to see a conversation I had carried in my gut for over a decade.

I have an identical twin. I always felt the constant pressure to prove that I was different, unique, worthy of being chosen. I didn't want to be better than her; I just wanted to be valued as an individual. I wanted to be loved as an individual, not as a joint venture that men could flip flop between whenever a few drinks blurred their vision. In the same way I felt written off by kids and teachers as just "one of the twins," I felt written off by the boyfriends who treated me like just another girl. I felt they couldn't see the difference, or didn't care to, like I had no unique value that stood out enough to honor monogamy.

These outdated conversations had hurt me for too long. When I was cheated on, I heard these voices slam against my mental door again. I could either believe the voices, or I could see the moment as God pushing these voices into my face and asking, "Hey kid, do you want to carry these with you anymore?"

Every relationship obstacle holds an opportunity. Will you complain about the "rash"? Or, will you hear the signal, acknowledge unhealthy internal conversations, and bring them into the light where you can see them, deal with them, and let them go for good? Patterns of insecurity, fear, despair, and defeat are opportunities to rebel against the voices that tell you that you are less. When these voices manifest in your relationship as tangible issues, you get a chance to look them in the face and say, "No thank you. I'm going on from here without you."

In the same way that healthy couples assume they are for each other and not against each other, you can assume that issues are here to help you, not to hurt you. Feelings are signals showing up to guide you, not to sabotage you. Your biggest relationship problems exist for you, not against you.

He Won'T Change, But You Will

Imagine the following: A client comes to me because she can't decide whether to stay with or leave her boyfriend. She spends hours motivating him toward his career. She goes to all his gigs. She supports him financially when work is slow. In return, he does nothing, except flirt with other women. Despite the one-sided relationship, she sees his potential. She talks to him about his potential, but every time they talk, he changes for a week or two at most. Then he inevitably goes back to his old ways. The potential exists, but only in doses. Every time she thinks about leaving, she hears an old voice in her head say, "Don't be so needy. He is as good as you will get. Be grateful for what you have. Other girls would be happy to have him." The voice sounds more like her mom's than her own.

Her mom worked three jobs to pay for her three little girls. When my client grew out of her clothes, she walked in ankle length pants for months before asking her mom to take her to the store. Being made fun of at school was better than the guilt trip she would receive if she asked mom for an appropriate size. The voice that said, "You should be grateful. You should feel guilty for wanting more," had been playing in my client's mind since childhood.

The outdated conversation kept her with men who were not treating her well. Some might call the pattern an issue. Instead, we approached the pattern as an opportunity, an opportunity to clear a conversation that she didn't want to carry into any new relationship. She broke up with him the next week, didn't feel guilty about it, and never felt more whole in her life.

The process wasn't pretty. We didn't photograph her trashcan of tissues and post it on social media. Courage is rarely pretty. Courage is the badass, un-photogenic choice that no- one else sees but us. She didn't come to me for a pat on the back. She came to me so that one day her kids could look in the eyes of a mother who had the backbone to run her own life, instead of being at the mercy of her emotions.

She had to face her habits, her fear, and her own expectations, but she eventually brought fear into the light where it could no longer run the show. Living in line with her truth required conscious and consistent decisions that sometimes appeared illogical, scary or uncertain. She continued to stay in the light when relationship baggage arose, changing the way she interacted with guilt, shame and doubt. It wasn't as easy as taking a pill, but she found her truth on the other side.

The Computer U.P.G.R.A.D.E

When the "Upgrade Now Available" window appears on your home screen, you don't freak out and say, "Oh my God, not again! I have so many bugs and fixes I can't believe it!" No. You click, "Run Upgrade Now." You watch as your computer enters a new level of functionality and ease. Upgrades never imply that the 1.0 version is bad. Upgrades imply that the 2.0 version is even better, with new systems, new software and new tools that will make the user experience more fun.

Relationship obstacles are like computer upgrades. You don't *have* to upgrade to 2.0, but you will have a tougher time downloading new and improved experiences if you don't. You are the computer, and as you evolve, you need to upgrade your internal software. You need to upgrade your perspectives and expectations to improve your current experience.

For a moment, bring to mind your biggest relationship obstacle. Tune in to how the obstacle feels in your body. Imagine that the tension you feel is the sound of an upgrade notification pinging against your heart. "Upgrade now available," the tension says. The ping isn't notifying you of something wrong you need to fix. The ping is saying, "Oh, man, do I have the upgrade of a lifetime. Would you prefer to hit upgrade now, later, or wait until tomorrow?"

How Culture And Evolution Keep You Stuck

Most women click "wait until tomorrow." The upgrades are better, but the outdated programs are familiar and wired into you by culture, biology, and psychology. Over the course of my private practice, I've observed five motivators that keep women trapped in old relationship patterns, and hesitant to upgrade:

Thanks culture: Its normal to judge certain patterns as "bad" and other patterns as "good". You tend to label patterns that create fear, insecurity or doubt as "bad" patterns. You slot fear-inducing patterns in the "upgrade later" category because you don't believe that an upgrade is even possible. Since you believe you can't upgrade, you learn to ignore the "bad" feelings, falsely thinking this will make you feel more of the "good". In chapters 03-09 you will learn that fear-based emotions like doubt and uncertainty are not bad at all, just misdirected gifts that are in need of an upgrade.

Thanks brain: Your brain is hardwired to give more attention to negative experience than positive. That is why you can have ten great dates and one bad date and write all men off as unavailable or selfish. You fixate on the ugly aspects of your relationship movie, fixated on what is not working instead of what is working. Don't worry, there is nothing wrong with you. Your brain is wired to focus on the negative because avoiding the negative keeps you safe. Unfortunately, focusing on the negative in relationships only makes it worse. Later in this chapter, I will suggest my favorite tool to teach your brain a new habit of focusing on the positive instead of the negative.

Thanks evolution: Your prehistoric ancestors needed to avoid danger in order to survive. The better they were at seeing dangers, the longer they would live. The faster they detected an obstacle, the faster they could avoid it, reproduce, and pass on those stressful genes to you. Your fight or flight response, which existed to keep them alive, now stays busy distracting you with your own relationship drama. That is why you are quicker to see relationship obstacles, than the equal number of relationship opportunities available. You will learn more about the hardwiring of your brain and the purpose of fear and stress in chapter 02. For now, go easy on yourself as you practice a new way to thrive.

Thanks media: Turn on any television and see that Americans are socially bred to think that difficult, codependent relationships are normal and inevitable. Why would you think to upgrade? The media normalizes drama. There is a saying that most men settle for a tolerable level of misery and call it happiness. You are not created to stay stuck in a tolerable level of misery. Your relationship is meant to be an expression of love, not a broken reflection of pain and insecurity.

Thanks patriarchy: All problems have emotional roots. Meaning, a breakup isn't bad unless you feel sad about it. Rejection isn't bad unless you feel hurt by it. Although emotions are inescapable, you are never taught how to navigate them. You are only taught which ones are good, which ones are bad, and how to ignore or stifle the feelings that you don't like. Here is a short lesson in patriarchy and its impact on the current state of emotional intelligence:

Emotions are feminine (a=b)
Femininity is weak (b=c)
Emotions are weak (a=c)

We should suppress weak things, like women and their natural gifts of emotion, intuition and empathy. You never learn the higher purpose of fear-based emotions. Instead of responding to how you feel by upgrading your situation, you feel stuck in a feeling for an indefinite season of time.

Your Feminine Gifts

You are not created to stifle and suppress your emotions like a 15th century man: tame and train what you do not understand. Each emotion has a life-enhancing role it wants to play; you just have to be courageous enough to face the unknowns, meet the wild you might not understand, and let each teach you a thing or two about how to love. When you face emotional and relational "obstacles" with a gentle attention, you find a storehouse of untapped gifts.

When you stop judging some emotional patterns as good and other patterns as bad, you find a freedom that "fixing" will never bring. In chapter 02, you will explore the purpose of "negative" emotions. In chapter 03, you will learn simple steps for upgrading your worst relationship issues into opportunities. In Chapter 04-10, you will use that formula to upgrade the seven most common emotions that sabotage relationships. You will learn how to respond to your feelings productively, proactively healing your relationship status as you go.

The Purpose Of Feelings

Do you battle with self-worth, perfectionism, doubt, boundaries, fears of neediness, control or people pleasing patterns? You've come to the right place. This book won't teach you how to get rid of these patterns. This book will teach you to respond to common obstacles as opportunities to step into your strengths. I'm writing this book to remind you that your relationship issues are actually signals reminding you of a very surprising opportunity, and opportunity to leave a legacy with your love life.

When I think of the potential opportunities lying in fear-based problems and feelings, I bring to mind Rudy. Rudy was my childhood nickname. Rudy has severe anxiety. She walks around with OCD from age 8-15. She hits light switches, closes and opens windows, and spends 30 minutes washing her face every day. She spends hours painting her bedroom ceiling with hypothetical death and disaster.

Fear, when I didn't understand her, wreaked havoc into my twenties. While doctors tried to prescribe pills to mute my angst, my parents and a few cutting edge practitioners helped me find the skill set in my fears, a skill set that was actually trying to empower me, my relationships and my future.

Think of emotions like employees. Every employee has a unique personality and skill set. All skills have a light and dark side. For instance, the same anxieties that plagued Rudy became skills I now use. Fear is good at being responsible, detail-oriented, and forward thinking. In the past, I used these skills to work myself into a panic. Now, I use the very same skills to plan adventures with my husband and fix issues when they arise. When you learn the healthy side of your emotions, you will eliminate the majority of the frustrations they currently create.

Before you move on to the next chapter, take a moment to scan your relationship story. When you face an obstacle, what is the main emotion you feel? For instance, if a partner betrays you, do you feel angry, or insecure, or do you feel ashamed for having chosen him? The emotion you tend to feel points to a skill set you're destined to use. The feeling, whether doubt, jealousy or fear, is waiting for you to embrace its healthy skill set.

I made a quiz to help you identify the core feelings at the root of your relationship frustration. You can take the quiz by visiting: www.TheUpgradedWoman.com. Simply enter your name and email, click subscribe, confirm your information, and take the quiz that comes with The Upgraded Woman Toolkit.

The quiz will identify which emotion is ready for an upgrade in your relationship. Then, Chapters 04-10 will guide you to hear the message this emotion is sending. Once you listen, you will cut relationship issues of at their core, so you can head into a more peaceful relational future.

The truth is, problem free relationships are possible if you view problems differently. What if problems are opportunities to upgrade? What if problems are simply side effects of misunderstood emotions? Would you see them as a problem? Probably not.

Understanding The Problem Doesn't Change The Problem

In order to utilize the healthy side of your emotional employees, you will have to make conscious choices, every day, around how you approach fear. It is easy to say you will make healthy choices right now, but in the heat of the moment, action becomes more difficult.

As you know, fear messes with your head, literally. When you focus on problems and worst-case scenarios in your relationship, you start to feel fear or doubt. Fear means that you have switched into a fight or flight response, which will make it nearly impossible to make calm, conscious decisions about how to act.

What is the main issue or obstacle you face in your relationship?
In this situation, what is the worst-case scenario?

When you think about this scenario, how much stress do you feel on a scale of 0-10?

Your brain can't tell the difference between what you think about and what you experience. That is why simply thinking about a problem and worst case scenario makes you more riled up than relaxed. Spending too much time attempting to understand relationship issues is counter productive when understanding it causes you stress. Stress sabotages your decision-making skills, which will perpetuate the problem. Before acting on a problem, use the following stress-reducing tools to put you back in a calm and productive frame of mind.

Tap Out Of Fear

The best decisions are conscious decisions, so I employ a few mindfulness techniques throughout the book to keep you calm while talking about somewhat fear-inducing issues. The most helpful techniques include body awareness, breath, meditation and Emotional Freedom Techniques. In the following chapters, I will include exercises that combine all four. You probably use these already, but here is a brief recap:

1. GET IN YOUR BODY

You have been taught to label fear-based emotions as bad. If you bring attention to your body, the feeling itself isn't bad. Feelings are physical sensations. Sometimes fear feels like a pressure in your neck or tingles in your stomach. Are tingles intimidating? Instead of labeling your fear, feel how the feeling shows up in your body.

For me, anxiety feels like someone is massaging my back with static. Not too shabby of a feeling. If I felt that in another context, I would label the tingles as excitement or anticipation. Feeling my anxieties on a physical level, instead of labeling them, helps me regain authority, and releases "negative" emotions more quickly.

Research shows that when you don't think about emotions, they only last 90 seconds. Ninety seconds! Over-thinking your emotions turns a 90 second chemical reaction into a year long pattern. Feelings aren't bad or good, they are just feelings trying to send you a message. Be brave enough to feel for 90 seconds. A true, un-judged feeling is one of the most beautiful gifts you can give yourself.

Where do you feel the fear in your body?

What colors, sensations, and descriptors do you imagine when tuning into the feeling?

2. BREATHE

Notice your breath right now. Did thinking of your worst-case scenario make you stop breathing? Hopefully, not. Breathing is the quickest way back to composure.

Take five second inhales and five second exhales. Take your breath a step further by dropping your jaw. Then drop your tongue to the floor of your mouth. Continue with the five second inhales. Your wise self is in there, she just needs some oxygen. After a few minutes of slowing your breath, imagine a person, place or thing that makes you grateful. Imagine love pouring from your heart on each exhale, and pouring back into your heart on each inhale. Now that you are in your rational mind, your worst-case scenario will feel less intimidating because it is in fact a worst-case scenario.

This simple breathing meditation was developed and studied by HeartMath. Their institute developed the breathing meditation as a way to mimic the brain waves of a Buddhist monk, or flow state. They tried all sorts of contraptions and modalities, and breath dropped participants into flow most quickly.

3. EMOTIONAL FREEDOM TECHNIQUES

If your worst-case scenario still makes you stressed, try the third mindfulness tactic: Emotional Freedom Technique aka EFT "tapping." I use EFT with clients who want to switch out of fear based thoughts and habits. Developed by psychiatrists and neuroscientists, EFT combines stress-reducing pressure points with exposure therapy. It brings you back to a calm state of mind so you can react to challenging situations in a productive way.

Like the name implies, Emotional Freedom Technique frees you from the side effects of fear, such as a racing heart, spiraling thoughts, and reactionary behavior, so you can respond to your situation in a calm and conscious way. Simply talk about your source of stress (exposure-therapy) while tapping pressure points on your face and neck (stress-reduction).

If you are a visual learner, you might benefit from the EFT how-to video included in the free toolkit. Find the video by visiting www.TheUpgradedWoman.com. Enter your name and email in the field. Once you confirm your info, you can watch the short tutorial included in the Toolkit. Let's begin.

TAP OUT OF STRESS EXERCISE

Pretend you are giving the pledge of allegiance. Begin massaging the point on your chest where you would normally place your hand. These pressure points tell the body you are safe. The point on the outside edge of your hand, known as the Karate Chop Point, has the same soothing effect. I suggest clients tap the pledge or karate chop point if they are worrying about a worst case scenario or recalling a stressful fight. Doing so soothes your nervous system and teaches your brain to stay calm, a better alternative to spiraling into fight or flight habits. Each time you tap, the more quickly you will regain composure when you face stressful scenarios in the future.

Using EFT is more effective when you get specific. Lightly tap your pledge point or karate chop point, and imagine your worst-case scenario. Think or say aloud, "Even though I'm afraid of this worst case scenario, I accept myself." Repeat this "setup statement" three times.

Then, begin tapping the EFT face points depicted as hearts below, which also can be found in the back of the book.

Use your pointer and middle finger to lightly tap each meridian point 7-10 times on either side of your face. Some people prefer to tap both sides of their face by using both hands. Others prefer to pick one side. The important part is to keep your mind focused on the specific problem you started with earlier. Staying focused while self-soothing teaches the brain to stay calm the next time this scenario arises in the mind.

As you tap the face points, repeat a "reminder phrase" in your mind or aloud to keep your mind focused on the issue, such as "this issue," "this worst case scenario," or feelings about the issue. Tap through 2-3 rounds while repeating your reminder phrases. Then, check in with your stress level. How is your stress level on a scale of 0-10? Most likely your stress level has lowered since you first check. If so, you're dropping back into your conscious mind.

When thinking of stressful situations, I encourage clients to really let their fear rip. Really exaggerate your worst-case scenario to the point of absurdity. Instead of saying "I'm afraid this will happen," say, "This will definitely happen!" There is no other alternative!" Exaggerating the worst-case scenario will make it feel unrealistic, because nine times out of ten, fear *is* unrealistic.

Does voicing the worst-case scenario feel weird? Of course. Does EFT feel weird? Yes. Weirder yet is walking around stifling your fears, which will end up sabotaging your life.

Talk And Tap

The reason I ask you to "tap" and talk in the following chapters is because talking doesn't change behavior. As you know, you can learn and learn and learn, and still make the same old decisions. Of course, you never do that, right? I want your behaviors to actually change, for good. I want you to stop dating the same people. I want you to stop dealing with the same insecurities. The only way to change your behavior is to change what motivates your behavior: your thoughts.

Tools like meditations and EFT communicate directly with the unconscious thoughts that control behavior. Instead of just understanding your problems, you will change your thinking, your reactions and your habits at the core.

Please, as you use this book, don't just read the exercises. Do the exercises. Take the time for yourself to tap and talk through your fears and thoughts, however odd it feels. Your future self thanks you.

What To Expect

I devote my career to guiding women to upgrade relationship issues by showing them how to navigate their emotions with mindful awareness. My intention is that you will respond to your worst moments and emotions with an empowered perspective. You will no longer react to fear and challenges with an attitude that has become so normal in Western culture. Your feelings, especially fear-based feelings, were never meant to dictate your life. They were never meant to be a weakness. They are, and always have been, your greatest strength. I'm writing this book to help you reclaim that strength.

Together we will learn chapter by chapter. The process will be new, some exercises will be challenging, but I will be with you all the way. If you get discouraged, remember the women in each chapter who are just like you. They face trust issues, heart-ache, and impossible decisions. They came to me after exhausting all options. Together, we tapped out of outdated patterns, and tapped into perspectives that empowered them to experience the love they always knew they deserved.

2

Feel The Feels

"That is why they are called feelings.
You are just supposed to feel them."
– Lynn Poinier

The Doctor placed my blood work in front of me. My endorphin levels were deep in the red zone. I looked at the key. Red meant suicidal. I was a freshman in college. While everyone came home winter break 15 pounds heavier, I had shed 15 pounds.

I felt like a walking coping mechanism. No one knew I was anxious. They just thought I had picked up a cocaine addiction or eating disorder while off at college. Nope, I had other drugs. I was addicted to an anxiety-inducing relationship cycle. Like a druggie who knows better, I kept taking hits off the same type of man. Then, I would take hits of the self-blame I had picked up from a few childhood traumas. The jealousy, inadequacy, anger, shame, and denial were running my life.

Therapists, hypnotherapists, doctors, psychologists treated my emotions like wild animals to tame, or best case scenario, kill. They prescribed pills, and books and programs that would put my emotions to sleep. They painted pictures of relationship health, confidence and contentment, if only I could master the art of removing my feelings. Since a lobotomy was not in my future, I decided to find my own way.

I found that the way through the chaos of my emotions was to understand that they were actually my biggest asset and strength. You might be wondering how. How are jealousy, insecurity, and doubt strengths? Well, it's all in how you use them – if you use doubt to settle, you bring darkness into your relationship. If you use doubt to increase your trust and take risks, you bring light into your relationship.

Have you ever gone on a date where the guy didn't call you back? Depending on the guy, no follow-up comes as a relief or as a disappointment. Has a man ever lied or cheated? Depending on the situation, betrayal is either soul crushing or a clear excuse to leave. Same situation, different feeling. One feeling makes the situation a problem. The other feeling makes the situation an answered prayer.

Unlearn The Lies

On my journey from relational hamster to relationship coach, I learned that feelings are at the root of all problems. It is your feelings about a situation, and how you respond to that situation which creates or heals the problem. The fear-based emotions you feel are not a sign of your brokenness. Fear is a sign of a strength, which is not trying to steal your peace, but save you from the relationship cycle you feel stuck in right now.

Yes, it might be hard to think of anger, judgment or fear as an opportunity, but trust me. My emotional cycles frustrated me until I learned that they were not out to get me, but help me. Was it easy to stop acting on my emotions in the dark? Heck no. Was it comfortable to feel my feelings all the time? Nope. Am I still consciously, every day, facing the decision to use my emotions in the dark or the light? Yes. But man is it freeing to look my husband in the eyes and know that we are not slaves to the dark patterns we both played out in our past.

The lies you are told about your emotions go something like this:

I should get rid of my emotions.
Some emotions are bad, like fear, doubt, uncertainty and anger.
Emotions are states of being. Example: I am insecure versus I feel
*   insecure.*
Ignoring my emotions gets rid of them.
Emotions are inconvenient.

Learning the truth about your emotions empowers you to attract and maintain a healthy relationship, a happy relationship, and dare I say, a relationship that frees you from the lies that don't deserve to run your love life.

The Truth About Your Emotions

All emotions are messengers

Negative emotions are a signal like hunger or pain. If hunger went away, you wouldn't know that you were starving. If pain went away, you wouldn't know that your curling iron was still on from last night. Emotions have a signal, a signal that serves. Getting rid of fear or other negative emotions is harmful to your body and your relationship.

All emotions are good emotions

Let us go back 195,000 years ago, when fear was necessary. Your first ancestors were crawling around on planet Earth, and unlike you, they lacked the luxury of a prefrontal cortex.

When they faced any threat, a soup of chemicals coursed through their veins, reminding them to fight enemies, run from danger, and freeze at the sight of threat. They didn't have the intelligent brain we have today that tells us how to handle challenges.

Today you are part of a bridge generation. You have your ancestors' highly developed fear response and your highly developed cognitive and spiritual adaptations. You are the first generation with tools to quiet fear's negative repercussions while maintaining fear's positive intentions.

Emotions are momentary

Emotions only last 90 seconds. Emotions bubble up and dissipate if you don't think about them negatively. When you think and worry about your emotion, you make it bubble up again. Think about your anger or insecurity less like a state of being and more like a cycle that you keep spin, spin, spinning with every thought.

Emotions get louder and stronger when you don't listen to their message

Ignoring emotions sounds like a good idea, but like a feisty teenager, ignoring them only makes them talk louder. My mentor Dawson Church was once asked, "Why don't your kids ever yell?" He calmly replied, as he does, "Because I listen to them the first time." He was explaining emotions. When you listen the first time, they don't have to come back with a vengeance later.

Emotions help us evolve

Emotions are only inconvenient when you don't speak their language. In early human history, fear's purpose was to help your ancestors fight, flee or freeze. Reacting with the three f's kept them alive and evolving. If you haven't noticed, life and relationships are very different than in the past. Reacting with fear no longer helps you. Nowadays, fear drives you into cycles of unhealthy and unconscious patterns. Carl Jung put it this way: "Until you make the unconscious conscious, it will direct your life and you will call it fate." When you become conscious to your relationship cycles, you will no longer feel fated to experience them. When you become conscious to your fear-based reactions, you will evolve your relationship's fate. Emotions still want to help you evolve, but they need you to interact with them in a 21st century way.

What Is Your Emotional Strength?

To begin to see your emotions differently, I'll teach you seven steps I call the U.P.G.R.A.D.E. Each step guides you out of common relationship issues that are emotionally based. Not only will you learn why emotions are at the root of common issues, but how to use those very same emotions in productive ways. While there are a plethora of emotions to cover, I will focus on the seven most common emotions that sabotage my clients' relationships: uncertainty, doubt, misused empathy, insecurity, shame, anger and judgment.

> Before you read this book, set an intention. If you could write your relationship into being, what would you include?
> How do you treat each other?
> How do you make each other feel?
> What do you both value?

How do you tackle conflict together?

How do you celebrate each other's successes?

Now ask yourself:

What is the main obstacle that is keeping me from this relationship story?

How does that obstacle make me feel?

Whatever emotion you feel in this situation, is most likely your core emotion. By the end of this book, your core emotion will become your core strength. The emotion is not showing up to hurt you, but to pull you out of your current obstacle, if you use its healthy side. The emotion you have is like any employee you hire. You have two choices. Let your employee stand by as you spiral deeper into fear patterns, or let her do the job she came to do: to help you navigate away from fear-based relationships and into a whole and healthy union.

Since emotions are multi-faceted, you might not know which feeling is at the root of your relationship pattern. Insecurity might appear like defensiveness. Anger might look passive and pent up. For that reason, it's important you check out the quiz included in the Toolkit. Your relationship will benefit from understanding all of your emotions, but getting to know your core emotion will help you maximize your greatest relational strength.

Access the Toolkit and quiz here: www.TheUpgradedWoman.com. Understanding your emotional strengths will rewrite the pages of your journals with a new story, a love story. When you understand anger, you are empowered. When you understand insecurity, you are rooted. When you understand doubt, you connect to a higher source that can pull you through any storm. When you embrace your emotions, and their positive purpose, you won't only upgrade your dating patterns, but patterns in your personal life, your health and your career.

3

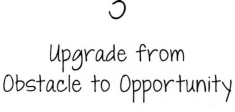

Upgrade from
Obstacle to Opportunity

♥ ♥ ♥

Fear does not want to sabotage you.
Fear wants to point out risks and keep you safe.

abrielle just found out that she was pregnant. I was the second
person to know, the first being the father, or possible father.
Gabrielle had just started dating her long-term boyfriend again
after a short break. They had been back together three months when
she woke up nauseous. The couple was excited, but Gabrielle had an
even more nauseating feeling that her boyfriend might not be the
biological father.

Gabrielle wanted to be honest and tell her boyfriend, but she was
terrified. She was afraid of being rejected, accused and alone. A voice in

her head said, "Don't tell him. He will call you a slut. He won't want anything to do with you." Fear convinced her to lie, saying, "If you tell him, you will hurt his feelings. He will think you are selfish. He will judge you and leave you." While fear chipped away at her peace, her intuition gnawed in her stomach and begged her to come clean. Fear was calling the shots, as fear tends to do when we don't understand it.

Gabrielle was doing what she had been taught to do her entire life, act on her emotions. Her parents, teachers, partners even encouraged her to act on her emotions by saying things like: "Do what feels right." What!? Please don't.

Sometimes what "feels right" is grabbing your man by the throat and catapulting that pointy knee of yours into a very sensitive region of his body. If Gabrielle acted on her emotions, she would lie about her situation. She would raise a baby who didn't know the truth about her dad. Her friends would wonder why the baby had blue eyes when they both have dark brown. She would settle, because she acted on fear, and fear told her to hide.

EXERCISE

What is your ideal relationship?

How would you like to feel in a relationship?

How would you like to act?

What is the biggest obstacle you face in experiencing your ideal?

Keep your answers in mind as we move through the U.P.G.R.A.D.E.

Gabrielle wanted to be in an open and supportive relationship. She didn't want to be afraid to tell the truth. She didn't want to face repercussions for her mistakes. She wanted to act with integrity, authenticity and courage. She felt incapable of living out these intentions because she was pregnant, in love with her boyfriend, and unsure if he was the real father. She felt afraid, uncertain, insecure and angry. She didn't know this when she called me, but her fear was not showing up to make her predicament worse. Her fear, like all feelings, was showing up to pull her out of her predicament.

Conditioned You vs. True You

There is a true you that is strong, brave, adaptable and courageous. There is a conditioned you that is fearful, nervous, apologetic and doubtful. The conditioned you has picked up how to live based on the past: past experiences, past partners, and parents. If you are reacting to life based on the past, you are settling for a life that is out of touch with your ideal future. The past is outdated. What applied to the last minute doesn't apply to the next. Yes, you can gain wisdom from your experience, but you should never confine your experience to yesterday. The true you is free to change constantly. Freedom doesn't need to apply old fears to new experiences. Fear makes you settle, and who wants that?

When I picked up the phone with Gabrielle, I knew that the issues and patterns she included on her intake form were not a result of her own choices, but her conditioned choices. Her true self is whole, perfect and enough, she just hadn't been taught how to listen to it. Her true self speaks to her through her emotions. Fear knocks from within, saying, "Hey, do you want to keep living like this, or do you want to make a new choice?"

Over the past six years, I've learned that you can't get rid of the doubt, or fear, or insecurity. You have to be honest about how you feel, so you can own the intention behind your emotion. Then and only then can you act intentionally toward yourself and your partner.

As I walked Gabrielle through the seven step U.P.G.R.A.D.E, we watched her problem turn into an opportunity. She not only felt peace about her obstacles but reconnected to an untapped inner power. This power would strengthen her as she navigated past obstacles and toward her higher intentions.

Your biggest obstacle is not your fear, but how you interact with your fears. The world tempts you to remove your fear as a way to remove your problems. Getting rid of fear-based feelings is the worst thing you can do. Feelings show up to protect you, and if you work with them, you will rise above the issues that caused them in the first place.

When Gabrielle journeyed through the seven steps, she was able to utilize the healthy side of fear to unapologetically own her past, confidently leave patterns behind, and freely create the relationship she had written off as impossible.

What are those seven steps?

The U.P.G.R.A.D.E Formula

Step 1: Unplug judgment aka Don't judge yourself for what is happening or how you feel

Step 2: Plug into message aka Listen to your feelings instead of stifling them

Step 3: Get honest aka Voice your deepest fears, so they don't sabotage you

Step 4: Remember your intention aka Focus on what you truly want, need and intend

Step 5: Act on Your intention aka Take action based on your intentions, not your feelings

Step 6: Develop your skills aka Take fear-based emotions and put them to good use

Step 7: Enjoy your saving grace aka Every emotion has an antidote you can use to stay on track

STEP 1
U: Unplug Judgment

The first step is to stop judging yourself for what you are going through right now.

Did you date a narcissist? No judgment. Are you unable to get over an ex? No judgment. Did you embarrass yourself by getting jealous for no reason? No judgment. Did you just act like a raging b*tch? No judgment.

When you face an issue, identify how you feel. Are you afraid, angry, worried, or uncertain? Do you judge yourself for feeling this way? Do you secretly think, "I *shouldn't* feel like this?" When you judge yourself for how you feel, you chain yourself to a past moment you can't erase. As you pull those chains into your future, the past inevitably repeats itself. Unplugging judgment will cut chains that tie you to the past, so you are free to decide on a new future.

Emotions Are Teenagers

Think back to when you were a teenager. What happened when your parent judged your hair color or your boyfriend? You rebelled. You became more unruly. Your emotions are hormonal teens. Literally, your emotions *are* hormones. When you judge yourself for how you feel, you only feel worse. Just as you would a teenager you loved, stop judging yourself. It's not like you chose the feeling, so why judge yourself for it?

Let's practice the U.P.G.R.A.D.E with an emotion that underlies every obstacle: fear.

Gabrielle feared she would be rejected if she told her boyfriend the truth. "I can't believe I even care this much. It sounds so pathetic saying it out loud. I'm usually so independent. If my clients knew I was this afraid to be alone, they would lose respect for me. I wish I didn't feel so dependent on this working out, or dependent on men in general!" She felt pathetic for fearing rejection. She judged herself for being weak. She was facing an impossible decision, and to make matters worse she was beating herself up for how she felt.

Don't beat yourself up. It is not weak or pathetic or shameful to fear loneliness. It is evolutionary.

Judge Evolution, Not Yourself

For generations, women depended on relationships in order to survive. Relationships ensured protection. They ensured provision. Women had to fear rejection because rejection could lead to death. The next time you feel tempted to beat yourself up for caring "too much" about a man, remember that evolution hard-wired you to care. Go easy on yourself as you learn a new way.

Learning a new way to respond to your feelings is the first step in transformation. When Gabrielle stopped judging herself for not feeling strong, she could give herself what she actually needed: compassion. The opposite of judgment is compassion. You don't have to like how you feel, but you can have compassion for yourself *as* you feel. While self-acceptance took time, unplugging self-judgment allowed Gabrielle to find peace in her impossible situation. She hadn't realized that the worst part about her situation was that she judged herself for being in it.

The first step in the U.P.G.RA.D.E is all about swapping your judgment for compassion. Once you have compassion, you are able to hear the message behind your core emotion, an emotion that wants to help you.

STEP 2

P: Plug Into Message

The second step is to plug into the positive message behind your feelings.

Like a computer update, emotions ping you with messages all of the time. It is your choice to listen to them or to ignore them until later. One reason you might not currently hear these underlying messages is because culture talks about emotions like identities, not signals.

Have you ever said the following? I am anxious. I am afraid. I am bitter. I am lonely. You are treating your emotions like identities, which gives them more power than they deserve.

Instead of saying, "I am <u>this emotion</u>." Say, "<u>This emotion</u> is sending me a message."

Interacting with emotions as messengers instead of identities rewires your mind to *listen to* them, instead of *acting on* them.

Fear Is A Flight Attendant

Fear and other fear-based emotions are like flight attendants. Her job is to inform and prepare you for worst-case scenarios. When she tells you about a hypothetical water landing, you can freak out and run off the plane or listen to her message. In the same way that water landings are only precautionary and very rare, fear's messages are mostly precautionary and rarely what actually happens.

The message behind all fear is safety.

When you hear fear, thank her for doing her job. "Why thank you fear. Thanks for reminding me that we could crash. How delightful. Can I put my headphones back in now?" If you take fear's message as truth, you will grab the emergency exit handle and create unnecessary chaos. The hope of any flight attendant is not that you actually act on what she says, but that you listen. Fear is no different. Listen for the rare chance that if a worst case scenario does happen, you will be prepared. Fear's hope is that you listen, not necessarily act.

My husband travels monthly. When I drop him off, at the airport, I think, "What if his plane crashes?" This thought lasts about half a second. Since fear's goal is to keep me safe, she reminds me of this worst-case scenario. She says, "I value your safety and your husband's safety. I want to keep his plane in the air, so let me remind you that it might crash." I listen to her message, but I don't need to give her a second thought if she is being unrealistic. Just like the flight attendant that will serve my man some coffee, her message is precautionary, not prophetic. This second step is all about listening to your feelings, and then putting your realistic headphones back in, and getting on your merry relational way.

What relationship scenario makes you afraid? In this situation, what does your fear want you to avoid? How is she trying to protect you?

Fear, and all your feelings have a message. As each hormonal emotion ideates about what could go wrong, you can make the adult decision about how to proceed. Instead of identifying with or stifling your fear-based feelings, you can listen. By courageously listening, you get honest about what you want, what worst-case scenarios you want to avoid, and what limitations you can realistically overcome.

STEP 3
G: Get Honest

The third step to upgrade from obstacle to opportunity is to get honest. Step three is all about the art of voicing your deepest fears. The fears that you can say aloud, are the fears that no longer have power over you. Getting honest about how you feel and what you don't want is the best way to move toward what you do want.

Despite sounding simple, step three can be the most challenging. Honesty demands that you own up and say what you need *even if* it inconveniences your partner. God forbid.

GET YOUR NEEDS MET EXERCISE
1. What is the worst-case scenario given my current issue?
2. Why does this scare me?
3. What do I need in order to feel safe?
4. What do I want?
5. What do I value?

Feelings like fear don't only tingle up your spine to inform you of worst-case scenarios. They bubble up to remind you of your deepest needs and values. Make a commitment to share your needs with your partner. Own what you want. Be honest about your values. If a partner feels threatened by your needs, wants or values, you can move on unapologetically.

Gabrielle had trouble with this step. She struggled because honesty demands that she declare her deepest needs. What? Is she allowed to have needs? Gabrielle is the oldest of four girls. Her entire life taught her to take care of her sisters and make her needs secondary. In her mind, needs are weak and selfish.

When I challenged Gabrielle to get honest, she admitted that she deeply feared raising the baby alone. Even worse, she feared that she would be seen as weak if she asked her boyfriend for help. What we resist persists, so we used mindfulness techniques to face her fears. She was able to reframe her belief from "her needs were inconvenient" to "her needs gave him an opportunity to rise to a worthy challenge." Only by getting honest could she reconnect to her needs and get her needs met! By outing her fear, she felt brave enough to ask her partner for help.

As usual, worst-case scenarios rarely come true. Her boyfriend hugged her, forgave her, and started building a baby crib. Obstacle thwarted. Health and wholeness spreading.

When you know the message behind your emotion, and get honest about what you want, only then are you able to see your intention clearly.

STEP 4
R: Remember Your Intention

Behind every "negative" emotion is a positive desire, the intention that drives most of your behavior. The fourth step is to remember your positive intention.

Alesha feels jealousy when her partner flirts because her intention is to be in a loyal relationship.

Briana feels angry when her partner ignores her because her intention is to feel respected.

Christie doubts whether she will ever get married because her intention is to find a husband.

Every obstacle you face is connected to a beautiful intention. Women who act with intention, instead of reacting to emotions, create the most fulfilling and problem-free relationship. For example, Gabrielle was afraid to tell her partner that the baby might not be his. When I first asked her what her intention was, she said, "To not have him hate me. To go back in time and not sleep with someone else."

Me: "Could you say what you do want instead of what you don't want?"

Gabrielle: "I want him to forgive me and to help me raise the baby."

Me: "Say your intention one more time, but in a way where you are making the final decision, not him."

Gabrielle: "I choose to raise the baby in a healthy family no matter what happened in the past."

Awesome. If Gabrielle focuses on her intention to create a healthy family for her baby, instead of "not having him hate me," she will have a much more productive conversation.

Now it's your turn:

What obstacle do you face?

This scares you because your intention is to _____

If necessary, rewrite your intention as positive and choice-driven. Once you remember your intention, you can take active steps toward reaching it.

STEP 5
A: Act On Your Intention

Once you know your intention, you can take the courageous fifth step, act.

There are many ways to react to relationship obstacles. The world teaches you to avoid what you don't want. I'm challenging you to run toward what you do want. The fifth step of the U.P.G.R.A.D.E is all about focusing on creating what you love, instead of avoiding what you hate.

Jane doesn't want to be lonely, so she acts desperate versus Joan who wants true love so she becomes the kind of woman she loves. Rochelle doesn't want her man to cheat, so she gets his email password and stalks his messages versus Rachel who wants to be with someone loyal, so she dates a man who has proven himself to be trustworthy. The latter examples create healthy relationships because they choose intentional action, not fearful avoidance.

The upgraded way of creating the relationship you deserve requires you act with intention, using your emotions as a compass, not a tiller.

REMOVE FEAR & AVOIDANCE FROM
YOUR RELATIONSHIP EXERCISE

1. **Rewrite your intention.**
   Gabrielle's Example: Create a healthy family for my baby.

2. **Brainstorm three ways you could reach your intended destination.**
   Gabrielle's Example: Lie to him so he doesn't reject us/ Downplay what happened so he doesn't get angry / Be honest, ask forgiveness and be the woman my daughter needs.

3. **Cross out options that are fear-based.**
   Gabrielle's Example: Lying to him is rooted in a fear that he won't forgive her mistakes. Cross it out.

4. **Cross out options that include avoidance.**
   Gabrielle's Example: Avoiding his anger sets her up to expect and then avoid his anger. Nix it.

Make a commitment to act on your true intention.

Gabrielle's Example: She set a date to take her partner out to dinner and tell him. Whether he chooses to stay or go, Gabrielle can feel peace that she took the healthiest, highest road.

Acting on a higher intention might be more difficult, but practice makes perfect. When you backslide into reactionary behavior, jump back to step one. Swap that self-judgment for self-compassion. Don't forget your tools. There are loads of extra mindfulness resources in The Upgraded Woman Toolkit, accessible at www.TheUpgradedWoman.com

Let's recap. Commit to not judging yourself for having feelings or (very human) issues. Commit to listening to the messages behind your feelings and the issues that trigger them. Commit to being honest about your fears, wants and needs. Commit to focusing on your positive intention instead of the fear-inducing problem. Commit to acting on what you do want instead of avoiding what you don't want. Now it is time for the fun part, step six.

STEP 6
D: Develop Your Skills

Anyone can become mindful of their intentions, but only the spiritually evolved can take what fear meant for bad and put it to good use! Every emotion comes with a set of skills. The point of step six is to recognize the skill-set that each feeling carries. Then you can commit to using those skills in healthier ways.

FIND THE SKILLS EXERCISE

When you feel fear in your relationship, how do you act?
How do you change emotionally, physically, mentally, relationally?

What skills or techniques are you using?

Can you think of scenarios when the same skills could help you?

You can access a printable checklist of each emotion's skills in The Upgraded Woman Toolkit mentioned earlier.

For example, fear is good at spotting obstacles and problem solving. Jealousy is good at comparing people against one another. Uncertainty is skilled at making pro and con lists. Sadness is skilled at remembering what it loves about someone. Every emotion has skills, skills that create healthy relationships if you use them in the light.

At its healthiest, fear is protective, detail-oriented, safety-seeking and creative. While these skills pull you down rabbit holes and paranoia spells, they can also pull your relationship into the light. You can use fear's ability to analyze problems to troubleshoot your partner's emotional issues. You can use fear's ability to brainstorm hypothetical scenarios to brainstorm creative solutions to your limitations. Get the idea?

Man, was Gabrielle creative. When Gabrielle felt fear, she created hypothetical realities in her imagination. Fearful thinking is more common in highly creative people. Creativity allowed her to make up hypothetical realities in her mind. In the dark, her hypothetical realities nearly sabotaged her relationship. In the light, her hypothetical best-case scenarios encouraged her to bravely tell her boyfriend the truth. Same skill. Different use.

Developing skills is easier said than done. The brain needs time to form new habits, but not as much time as you might think. I'd like to encourage you with a nerdy fact. Research has shown that the brain needs only 21 days to turn a new decision into a perpetual habit. If you have spent 21 years with your current habits, give yourself at least 21 days to develop healthier dating habits. Decide on how you want to act, and give yourself at least 21 days to practice.

I obviously must suggest that you practice the previous steps for 21 days. If you need accountability, you can participate in my five week program. If six steps seem difficult to remember in the heat of the moment, the seventh step is for you. One more to go!

STEP 7
E: Enjoy The Saving Grace

Each emotion has what I call a saving grace, the antidote to employ when roadblocks inevitably arise. The saving grace will be your quick reminder to approach your situation in the healthiest way possible. The cheat sheet mentioned above includes the saving grace that will help when you are feeling one of the seven most common emotions.

The worst thing you can do when feeling afraid is nothing, except to ruminate down the Alice and Wonderland hole of mental chaos. When you feel afraid, the best you can do is to take action. When you take action, you prove your worst fears wrong and prove just how strong you are at your core. For this reason, the saving grace of the emotion fear is action.

Every Woman Should Be A Buffalo Woman

Every animal has symbolic meaning. For me, the buffalo symbolizes courageous action. When a storm approaches, the buffalo is the only animal to head directly into the rain. While all the other animals run away, the buffalo heads into the eye. The buffalo knows that by taking action, it will get through the storm more quickly.

Instead of waiting in paralysis until her boyfriend brought up the fact that the baby might not be his, Gabrielle took action. She had to head straight into her relational storm. Before she acted, she used the detail-orientation skills of fear that we learned about in chapter 02. She made sure she was eating at her boyfriend's favorite restaurant and on a day when his workload was light. Thank you fear for those awesome techniques. Just like the buffalo, the storm didn't end her. The storm taught her that worst-case scenarios rarely come true and that obstacles can strengthen and evolve her partnership.

What's Next?

Depending on your personality, you will respond differently to different obstacles. You might be quick to judge or blame or worry or lash out. As you now know, these emotions are not bad. They are opportunities to reach new levels of wholeness and leave a legacy with your choices.

In the following chapters, you will learn to move seven emotions out of the dark and into the light. By taking each emotion through the U.P.G.R.A.D.E, you won't let emotions run your relationships. You won't let insecure feelings land you with the wrong men. You won't let doubt make you ignore your intuition. You will enter relationships from an evolved and empowered place.

Since most women tend to relate to relationships through one or two emotions, remember to take the quiz included in the toolkit. Once you identify your core emotional response, you can focus on maximizing the strengths your personality is designed to master.

Access the quiz here: www.TheUpgradedWoman.com

How To Read This Book

By category: The emotions I refer to in the book are grouped into three categories: Complicated, Single, and Dating. I group the emotions based on when the emotion shows up on the relationship journey most often. For example, insecurity arises in single women, but it obviously rears its head within a relationship as well. I created the categories to help you find emotions more easily.

By your emotional strength: Once you take the quiz, you can head directly to the chapter that matches your emotional strength, learn about how you might be misusing the emotion, and then upgrade it.

Read the whole darn thing: I recommend this approach. Every emotion is connected in a web of experience. You might not resonate with anger, but understanding it will reveal a side of you that might be waiting to heal and help your relationship. If you don't resonate with an emotion, read it on behalf of a partner, or future partner. Understanding the emotions that drive your partner will help you approach conflict consciously and compassionately.

Do the exercises: This book contains many exercises. Don't just read them; do them! At some points, I lay out some pretty ugly beliefs. If you are not using the mindfulness tools I suggest, you could reinforce old beliefs. If you want to take the exercises to the next level, download the free toolkit. The toolkit includes a how-to video, cheat sheet and a 30-minute strategy session with me. No matter where you are, I can walk you through the blocks you encounter as you journey through the book.

Download the U.P.G.R.A.D.E CHEAT SHEET: Located in the free offer at the back of the book, the cheat sheet organizes each emotion, its healthy and unhealthy side, and the saving grace that will pull you out of the seven most common relationship obstacles.

Don't Mind The Pronouns

The majority of my clients are heterosexual females. When I lay out writing prompts and mindfulness exercises I refer to the reader as *she* and her partner as *he*. This choice is for simplicity purposes only.

On that note, let's begin by exploring the emotions that arise when love gets complicated. Since you are an organized, entrepreneurial woman, you value clarity and control. Unfortunately, matters of the heart don't follow the same rules as matters of business. One of the most paralyzing emotions my clients come to me seeking to understand is uncertainty. If uncertainty is stealing your relational peace, then chapter 04 is for you.

Before you begin, I'd like you to turn the page and make seven commitments for yourself and the future of your relationship.

An Upgraded Woman's 7 Commitments

Before you embark on this journey, make seven commitments on behalf of your healthiest self and you healthiest relationship. There is science to back up the importance of each commitment, but I'll spare you the details.

1. **Respect the difference between thoughts and feelings**: Saying, "I feel like I should stay with him," is not a feeling. That is a thought. A feeling is, "freeing, shrinking, tense, open, safe, embarrassed." Those are feelings. If someone makes you feel small and tense, and like you "should" be with them, they might not be the right person for you. You might feel angry or sad in moments, which is normal. Focus on the pervading feeling in your day-to-day relationship.

2. **Respect the difference between your emotions and their emotions**: Sometimes you will feel awkward around a person because you are finding your self-worth in their opinion. Other times, you won't understand why you feel awkward around them. In these moments, you might be picking up on their emotions. Maybe *he* feels insecure. Maybe *he* feels awkward. Do a gut check. Take a breath. Let him do him and you do you.

3. **Give yourself permission to not be perfect.** Nothing you learn in this book should be used to beat yourself up. If you get anything from this book, get this: Don't judge yourself! The less you beat yourself up about your choices, the less gun-shy you will be the next time you have to make a choice.

4. **Use your wisdom to love your partner, not to preach to him:** You will be tempted to preach to your partner about what you learn. This is not your job. If you are telling him as a way to love him better, go ahead and share. If you are telling him as a way to prove why he is wrong, please refrain.

5. **Pursue joy:** When you are single, pursue joy. If you are dating, pursue joy. If you don't know if you should be with someone, choose to have joyful moments with them anyway. Then, you will at least be having a good time while you are learning and growing together. If you know you shouldn't be with someone, and you are stringing him along, that is a different story. If you honestly don't know, have fun with him as you gain more clarity. Joyful honesty is the best policy.

6. **Enjoy being wrong:** What if your deepest fears, deepest worries, deepest points of insecurity, were proven wrong tomorrow? What if you never thought you would meet someone who was smart, and sexy, and caring, and driven, and then tomorrow you met someone who met all of those standards. Embrace the joy of being proven wrong.

7. **Surrender your expectations:** When you don't have expectations about what will happen, you can't limit yourself. Set an intention for who you want to be in every moment and let yourself live in the reality that no matter what expectations you have, you might surpass them. If you want one expectation, expect that all your expectations will be surpassed.

PART TWO
It's Complicated

"An invisible red thread connects those who are destined to meet regardless of time, space or circumstance. The thread may stretch or tangle, but it will never break."
– Asian proverb

4

Uncertainty: Is this Fear or Intuition?

♥ ♥ ♥

Uncertainty shouldn't leave you feeling confused or unwise.
Uncertainty is a sign to surrender control and enjoy the ride.

A va was a business owner, business starter, freelance designer, writer, educator, and in the middle of a decision she couldn't make: Is he right for me? She knew how to annihilate a to-do list, prioritizing best options and courses of action, but when it came to her relationship, man did she feel uncertain. She tried to checklist her way to answers with a pro and con list. Didn't work. She hadn't told me about all the sisters and friends and coworkers she had asked for advice, but I could hear them behind the question mark tone of her voice when she asked if I would take her on as a client, and help her find answers. One part of her hesitated to call him boyfriend because something in her wasn't feeling the spark. Another part of her hesitated to end the relationship because the last time she followed a spark it left her burnt and bitter.

I decided to ask Ava a few questions.

"So Ava, what is at stake if you don't make the right decision?"

"Excuse me?"

"Well, say you choose him, and ten years from now you have an epiphany and realize you did it all wrong, that he is not the guy for you. What is at stake?"

"I don't know."

"What if you broke up with him, and then looked back in ten years and realized that he was the best guy you could ever get? What would be the worst case scenario?"

"That is what I don't know. I don't know if I'll regret staying with him or regret leaving him! I just want someone to tell me what to do."

I think Ava wanted me to whip out my crystal ball so she could know with 100% certainty if she was making the right decision. Everything else in her life was clear and controllable, why couldn't her relationship feel the same?

There was a part of Ava that already knew the right choice. Her ego was just too scared to say it aloud because it might turn out to be wrong. Ava had lost access to her true self because the sound of her friends' opinions, her fears, and her past choices hummed too loudly to make the brave choice.

The brave choice is to follow the voice that begs you to never settle. After we worked through her options and reconnected to her truth, she realized that no matter what choice she made, she would be okay. She no longer saw her choice as life or death, but a momentary decision that she could reroute. She stopped worrying about if she was making right and wrong turns and started enjoying who she was as she traveled. Detours, in the end, are the perfect place to let go of an agenda and explore who you are on your journey.

The women I work with are leaders, organized and success-driven, but where they feel certain in their career, they feel uncertain in relationships. The majority of my coaching work with women has to do with reclaiming the intended purpose of uncertainty.

Reacting to uncertainty the way the world reacts, in the dark, will leave you feeling paralyzed in the face of a future you cannot control. You will doubt yourself, flipflop between decisions, and worry that you will have to live with the repercussions of "wrong" choices.

UNCERTAINTY IN DARK	UNCERTAINTY IN LIGHT
Stuck in confusion and lack of clarity	Surrenders to the uncontrollable
Confused by friends' and families' opinions	Embodies the identity we can control
Incapable of deciding; paralysis	Trusts self to make right choice
Stresses about the right choice	Discerns the difference between right and wrong choice
Can't make a decision	Sees pros and cons easily
Worries about making the wrong choice	Confidently makes leadership decisions despite potential failures
Worries about looking back at choices with regret	Surrenders control over past decisions
Confuses fear and intuition	Makes informed, truth-centered decisions
Ask friends for advice	Follows inner compass for advice

Reacting to uncertainty in the light will lead you back to a deep sense of control and clarity over who you are and what you want. You will stop worrying about your choices, and start focusing on who you will be as you make each choice. Unless you like staying in a constant tail chase toward the "right" choice, you can upgrade uncertainty by pairing it with its antidote, surrender.

When you upgrade uncertainty, you will be able to confidently make a decision, even if you don't have all the answers. You will have patience, with yourself, and hope in timing. You will stop beating yourself up for past decisions and look forward to relationship crossroads in the future as an opportunity to embody your deepest values.

Unplug Judgment

Remember, your lack of answers is not the main problem. The tendency to judge yourself for not having all the answers is the bigger problem. Whether your decision involves a breakup, a hard conversation, or a new level of discipline, you can begin by giving yourself some much-needed compassion. You don't know what to do just yet, and that is perfectly okay.

Ava valued clarity and discernment. Of course she beat herself up for not knowing the right decision. When I asked Ava what was wrong with not knowing the right choice to make, she impressed me with her blunt vulnerability.

Ava: "I hate making the wrong choice. I'd feel so selfish and stupid for making a mistake."

Me: "What is bad about making a mistake?"

Ava: "It means I'm stupid, and disconnected."

Me: "Disconnected from what?"

Ava: "I should be able to hear my intuition, and I clearly can't. Last week I woke up certain that I should end it with him. Then this morning, I woke up feeling certain that I should give him a chance. I don't want to be that kind of person."

Ava was less frustrated with her situation than she was with herself. There was nothing wrong with Ava's uncertainty, except that she was judging herself for feeling it. Uncertainty made her feel out of control, which made her scramble for control by finding the "right" answer.

Addicted To Control

You probably hate feeling uncertain because the ego craves control. Like all addicts, your ego tries to remove obstacles to control, uncertainty being one of them. The ego will say, "Control tastes good. Control is good for you. Certainty is good for you. Uncertainty is for losers." The ego will trick you into thinking that removing uncertainty is the solution. You will attempt to lasso uncertainties because the more certain you feel, the more satisfied the ego becomes. While the ego obsesses over controlling uncontrollable scenarios, like decisions that simply need more time, it will distract you from the very thing you do have control over. (More on that later.) All this to say, if you need an excuse to not judge yourself for seesawing between control issues and a lack of answers, I hereby give you permission to blame your ego.

Speaking of scapegoats, three cultural beliefs feed your ego's addiction to certainty.

1. **There is always a right and wrong answer:** Culture teaches you that certainty is better than uncertainty. From the first time you raise your hand in school, you learn that having an answer is better than not having one. If a teacher calls on you and you freeze, you feel inadequate for not knowing. Having the right answer is glorified. The truth is that there is not always a right and wrong answer.

2. **Certainty is a sign of wisdom:** Culture is rich with "experts" who seem to be certain about everything. Experts don't have questions. Experts don't have unknowns. Experts don't feel uncertain. Ha! Of course experts feel uncertain. Certainty is not a sign of wisdom or discernment. Let your lack of answers remind you that you are created to question. Questions lead to true wisdom.

3. **Being certain about a course of action is responsible:** Let's break this cultural belief down. Responsible means reliable and dependable. How many times has your friend been certain about a guy you were dating? Of these times, how often was her opinion dependable? Not often. Feeling certain about a decision is not the same as making the responsible decision, let alone the right one. The next time you feel uncertain, reconnect to the truth: The most responsible choice is to surrender control of outcomes that were never yours to control in the first place.

Research reveals that at any given time, you have conscious awareness of 10 percent of your reality. If you feel uncertain, remember: You can only be certain about 1/10th of what is right in front of your face. Be patient, accept your uncertainty, and then plug into the positive message behind this emotion.

Plug Into Uncertainty's Message: Where Have I Lost Control?

One of my favorite episodes of Seinfeld is the Serenity Now episode. George's dad, Frank, starts ferociously yelling, "Serenity now," whenever he feels stressed. He learned the tactic from his therapist. His therapist's tip comes from the Serenity Prayer. You've heard it before, but here it is for your reference:

God grant me the serenity to accept the things I cannot change;
courage to change the things I can;
and wisdom to know the difference.

The positive message behind uncertainty is to remind you what you *do* have control over.

Since the ego, or conditioned self, likes control, uncertainty tempts you to take control. For example, you might not know if he is the one, so you try to gain control by asking friends and reading books and seeing therapists. Your ego is trying to gain control by securing a "right" answer. Despite the temptation, don't respond to uncertainty by focusing on what you don't have control over. You don't have control over seeing the future, over your partner's evolution, his behavior toward you, or his feelings for you. Accept the things you cannot control and have the courage to change the one thing you can, yourself.

Release Certainty To Find It

The wise and conscious woman in you knows that just because control feels good, doesn't mean you need to be in control of everything. In fact, you aren't created to be in control of everything. You can't control your lack of answers. You can't control your mixed emotions about what to do. You can't control your uncertain future. You can only control the attitude you have in the face of uncertainty. Will you be a woman who makes choices based on her deepest intentions or her deepest fears?

The next time you feel uncertain about a tough decision, hear uncertainty say,

"Hey! Over here! I need answers! I need to feel certain before I feel at peace."

Politely reply, "I know you like certainty. Sorry, but I can't be certain about the future. I can't be certain that everything will work out. I can only

be certain about who I will be when the uncertain future arrives. I am certain that I will act with integrity. I am certain that I will take care of myself. I am certain that …"

If you are having a hard time feeling at peace with the uncertainties in your relationship, fear might be confusing your choices. Before you can find peace, you will have to expose the fears hiding underneath your current options.

ASSESS YOUR OPTIONS EXERCISE

1. Where in your relationship do you feel uncertain?
2. What are your options?
   Option A:
   Option B:
   Any other options? Give yourself more than two choices.
   Option C, D, E.
3. If you don't choose at all right now what could happen?
4. If you had to choose today, what could happen?

Underneath each option is a pressure to choose the right one. If there wasn't a pressure, you would feel at peace with your uncertainty. I don't know about you, but I make wiser decisions when I tap out of fear and pressure, and into a more inspired perspective. Take a few soothing exhales. I suggest you use mindfulness strategies or tap the stress-reducing pressure points depicted in chapter 02 to ease your mind. As you self-soothe, the pressure will become less intimidating. You will slip into an, "I trust the process" mentality that fosters empowered decision-making.

After Ava and I worked through her options, she realized that her fight or flight was acting like there was a gun to her head. Her conditioned self told her that if she made the wrong choice, she would never get another chance to be with someone better. As you have painfully learned, no matter how many times you dot your "i's" and cross your "t's", you still might end up regretting a decision. Hindsight is 20-20.

All you can do is hear your uncertainty, hear its warnings about the possible outcomes you want to avoid. Then make the best decision you possibly can based on what you can control. What can you control? Who you are and who you want to be as you make the decision. Then forgive yourself if your choice leads you down an uncomfortable path. Speaking from experience, the worst case scenarios waiting at the edge of each option rarely come true.

All you can do is surrender your future to more optimistic hands. Sorry if this information is not soothing, but fear's discomfort is fertile ground for growth and self-trust. Uncertainty begs you to make decisions based on your highest intentions and needs, instead of your deepest fears and weaknesses. It also challenges you to drop the pressure, and give yourself the time you deserve to make an informed choice.

When uncertainty pipes up, respond by saying, "Thank you uncertainty. I want clarity and control too, but I need more time, more information or more patience before I can choose what is best for me. The only thing I can control is the person I choose to be and how I treat myself as I decide."

No harm can come from patience and surrender. The worst that can happen is that you rush to a decision. Then, you can always make a new choice. Instead, get clear about who you want to be as you wait for clarity. Will you be someone who stays with a partner because you are afraid there is nothing better? Will you be someone who leaves a partner because you are afraid of what your friends think of him? Will you be someone who pressures yourself to choose before you are ready? You have choices.

Get Honest

Ava's voice strained my phone with angst as she rifled off her options. I stopped her to ask some questions.

Me: "Hey Ava, what are your choosing between right now?"

Ava: "Well, what I just told you. Do I stay with him or leave him?"

Me: "Okay, and what is the worst case scenario if you stay with him?"

Ava: "I will realize that I settled and that God had someone else for me, but I didn't wait for him. I'll make it work but I'll be unhappy."

Me: "Great. And what is the worst-case scenario if you leave him?"

Ava: "I might start dating other people, and realize that no one is as good as him. I'll realize I took him for granted and let my baggage, or some warped self-sabotage, tell me that he wasn't good enough when really he was. I'll have to watch him get married to some other girl and I'll end up alone."

If you are facing a decision that feels life or death, it means you are no longer making a rational choice, but choosing between two worst case scenarios. Lose-lose situations rarely end well.

YOUR HONEST OPTIONS EXERCISE

Rewrite your options. Next to each, write what the worst-case scenario is if you choose it.

OPTIONS	WORST CASE SCENARIOS

When Ava got honest about her uncertainty, she saw that she wasn't actually choosing to stay or to leave. She was choosing between the lesser of two evils: Being really unhappy in a marriage vs. watching the love of her life married to another girl. Of course she had a hard time deciding.

If you don't get honest about your uncertainty, you live in limbo between two hells. When you get honest, you bring your fears into the light, where they disappear like the shadows they are. You won't feel desperate to make a decision. You will open up to insight, something that is unavailable in an extreme fear state.

Most of my clients write their worst-case scenarios and realize that the likelihood of them happening is low. Putting pen to paper is a simple way to put your fearful thoughts to rest. Get honest about the worst case scenarios that are at stake, and then you will have an easier time making a choice that reflects a higher intention.

Remember Your Intention

Look at your source of uncertainty, and you will find that you are trying to control an uncontrollable factor. You are like a bride who tries to control the weather on her big day. She forgets that she can only control the dress, the dance and who she dances with when the day actually arrives.

If your intention is to make the right choice, then you need to focus on what choices are in your hands.

The intention behind uncertainty is to feel certain about making the right choice.

Look at your options. Write down which aspects of your option you have control over and which you don't have control over. Then list choices you have in the areas you *do* have control over. Let me explain.

Ava can't be certain if she is with the right person. That is okay. She can surrender control, and take one step at a time. What can Ava be certain about? What she wants in a man. She is certain that she wants someone who respects his mom, who has drive, and who treats her like a priority, amongst other things.

Ava does not have control over:
If her boyfriend will make her feel a spark.
Whether he will end up being less than she expected.
Whether another man will come along and be better than him.

Ava does have control over:
How she acts despite her emotions.
If she wants to choose to stay with someone who doesn't satisfy her.
If she wants to stay with a man who makes her fantasize about someone else.

Ava can choose to stay with him, despite dissatisfaction. She can choose to be with him for another month and then decide. She can be certain about these choices. And then, when she does make a final decision, she can choose to trust that she did the best she could.

Act On Your Intention

When Ava acted on her emotion, she wavered between staying or leaving. She was too afraid to make a move, too afraid to face the consequences. She stayed confused, unclear, and made decisions based on avoiding being alone.

Ava had a choice: Act on her uncertainty or act on her intention to make the right choice.

Ava wanted sparks. It wouldn't be "right" to spend her life feeling disappointed that he didn't ignite them. She didn't want to settle. It wouldn't be "right" to choose him as a way to avoid loneliness. She wanted him to change. It wouldn't be "right" to say yes to a man who she constantly wanted to fix. As she honored and acted on her intention, she elevated her definition of the "right" choice. Making the right choice was no longer a shallow desire to control her future, but a profoundly loving act of kindness to herself and her partner.

TAKING CONTROL EXERCISE

Since you can't feel certain about the right decision, get certain about how making the right decision will make you feel. Imagine a guru comes to tell you your whole future. Imagine that you finally feel 100% certain that you are making the right choice.

1. What fears fade?
2. What changes about how you show up in your relationships?
3. How do you finally get to feel?
4. Who do you get to be as a woman and a partner when you feel this way?

Now for the punch line question:

5. Do you have to wait for a certainty before you can be, feel or act this way? Or, can you be this woman right now?

Since Ava wants to be a woman that lives with trust, she chose to break up with her partner. Instead of feeling afraid that she would end up alone, she felt like the break up was an act of faith: "Hey universe. I know you won't leave me hanging."

Develop Your Skills

Imagine all the women out there who couldn't care less if they make a wrong choice. They don't care if they make a foolish choice. No, not you. You care about making the right choices. You care about doing what is best. The majority of people don't care, and they have their life to show for it. Uncertainty, while she may be the bane of your existence, carries a skill-set. If you constantly feel uncertain, it means you care about being your best self and experiencing your best life.

If you feel uncertain, you are part of a shrinking class of humans who value responsibility and discernment. While the world continues to fly by the seat of their pants, you tread with caution, taking wise steps. Below, check out some skills that come along with the uncertainty. Brainstorm scenarios when you can use each skill to help your relationship status.

When you feel uncertain, breathe and remember: Uncertainty is given to you so you can remember to surrender. You can control your attitude, your intentions and your highest good all you want,

Skill	Creates problems when	Creates health when
Control	You control your partner, his habits, and how your relationship runs	You use that skill to plan fun weekend dates and diligently pursue personal values
Critical thinking	You downplay your feelings with thinking	You balance logic with intuition
Seeing pros and cons	You try to change cons you can't control	You make informed decisions about your career and relationship plans
Can see potential obstacles	You worry and nitpick	You prepare for obstacles and move ahead with faith
High standards	You set high unreachable standards for your partner	You set high standards of self-excellence and create daily habits to journal and debrief on progress

but surrender the outcome, the opinions, and the evolution of your partner.

Enjoy The Saving Grace: Surrender

I love control. I am a type A control freak. Since like attracts like, I tend to work with other type-A women. If you never fall beneath A+, making a decision that feels like a failure might make you lose trust in yourself. When you face a relationship crossroad and "failing" feels possible, you might spiral into conditioned ways of seeking control.

When you close this book, don't fall into that trap. Or, get in touch with me if you do. Use certainty's saving grace: Surrender. Ask yourself, what is within my control? What is out of my hands?

You will inevitably face a decision where you feel uncertain. You can respond in two ways.

Conditioned response: I don't know what to do! Maybe I should ask friends! I messed up last time.

Upgraded response: You breathe. You realize that you have as much time as you give yourself. You connect to the one thing you can control, yourself. You stand in full trust that no matter what choice you make, you will show up for yourself, choosing again, and giving yourself grace if you make a "wrong" turn.

Roadblocks On The Route To Surrender

You will feel certain he's the one, and then he won't call you back. Be honest about what you can and cannot control and surrender accordingly: You can control what attitude you take in the face of rejection. You can't control if he asks you out on another. You can control if you love yourself despite his choices. Surrender what you cannot control.

You will need to make a decision: Give yourself permission to not be certain. The best antidote to feeling plagued by uncertainty is to let yourself off the hook. Tell your fight-or-flight mind: We don't have to make a decision right now. Women, especially creative women like you, work best when you aren't under pressure. Surrender timing.

Your friends will give you conflicting advice: You will always feel uncertain if you seek answers outside of yourself. Others' opinions are their projections and will muddle your ability to have trust and confidence in yourself. Surrender external validation and seek validation from within.

You will want to look to the past for advice: Fear will take past evidence and use it to prove your deepest fears true. Don't be fooled. The past does not repeat itself, so stop looking to the past for answers. A quick look at life will show you that new and miraculous things happen all the time. Some of the most miraculous encounters happen when you have absolutely no control. Surrender the past.

Enjoy The Ride

Surrender lets you enjoy your relationship instead of controlling it. Surrender gives you time to meet the person you are with before having to predict and control where you will be in ten years. Uncertainty was never given to you so you would control the uncontrollable. She exists so you can surrender control and enjoy the ride.

When you do muster the courage to surrender control, you encounter another emotional obstacle: Doubt. If you have ever doubted yourself, your partner, or men in general, the next chapter is for you. Doubting that your relationship can get better is not so much of an issue as it is a beautiful chance to upgrade.

5

Doubt: I Don't Want to Settle

💜 💜 💜

Doubt will pretend it is truth, but doubt is
asking you to trust your gut and take a risk.

Alanna was climbing toward thirty and the pickings were slim. She was facing a gut-wrenching realization that what she wanted didn't exist. She had been seeing a really nice guy, emphasis on nice. Her friends liked him. Her sister liked him. She wanted to like him, but a small voice kept telling her there was something more. Despite the voice, she didn't leave. By the time she called me, she had ignored her intuition for so long that she no longer recognized its voice.

Me: What do you want?

Alanna: I'm not sure. I thought he was what I wanted, but apparently not.

Have you found yourself in a situation where you can't tell the difference between your fear and intuition? Have you wondered if the relationship you want is realistic? Have you bargained to meet him sooner? Have you started to give more men a chance, even though you feel nothing for them? Doubt will do this to you, leave you feeling disillusioned, confused, selfish, and out of time. Until you face the obstacle in the light, doubt will make you settle for the wrong man before the right one has time to find you.

DOUBT IN THE DARK	DOUBT IN THE LIGHT
Worries if relationship goals and dreams are selfish	Trusts that reaching goals will inspire others and increase generosity
Feels stupid for getting excited	Trusts timing and desires
Settles as a way to avoid disappointment	Sets high expectations and takes risks despite past disappointment
Focuses on temporary obstacles	Focuses on long-term dreams and internal compass
Loses trust in self and others	Reveals opportunity to deepen trust
Loses trust in Divine	Reveals opportunity to deepen trust in the divine
Stops hoping because of other's opinions	Keeps hoping despite being thought of as crazy
Becomes jaded and pessimistic	Becomes inspired and intuitively led

If you are in a complicated situation, if you second-guess your intuition, if you don't want to settle, you are in the right place. My goal in this chapter is to teach you to trust your heart's desires. Doubt doesn't have to have such ugly repercussions, so let's upgrade doubt into its counterpart, courage.

As you move through the next seven steps, you will learn the difference between your fear and your finely tuned intuition. You will be able to honor red flags when you see them. You will develop patience as you wait for the one. You won't waste time on dates that go nowhere. You will develop the courage to trust again.

Unplug Judgment

When Alanna called me, she had just ended a two year relationship. Her friends loved him, her family loved him, but she couldn't make herself love him. Even though nothing was wrong, something didn't feel quite right. She broke it off, but a few months later she was in doubt. Had she let her baggage ruin a perfectly fine relationship? Had she made a mistake? Should she ask him to take her back?

You've probably been here. You make a decision. You trust yourself, momentarily. Moments later, you question if the anchor you felt pulling you to leave was real. To make matters worse, you might beat yourself up for feeling all the doubt.

Alanna wanted a final decision. She wanted to trust her decision. What she really needed was to go easy on herself. When she did, she learned that her doubt was an important step. Her doubt was revealing the fear that kept her from trusting her intuition in the first place.

Doubt is just intuition attached to fear. Fear + Intuition = Doubt

TRUST YOUR INTUITION EXERCISE

Let's walk through three scenarios that make you hesitant to trust your intuition. As you read each scenario, write down memories from your own life that relate.

1. **You followed your intuition and it let you down.**
   Example: You trusted your intuition in college, and you ended up dating a jerk.
2. **You learned that what you want is not realistic.**
   Example: Your mom told you that finding a man with morals, a fat paycheck, and a similar spiritual life is unrealistic.
3. **Your intuition is leading you down an inconvenient or unattractive path.**
   Example: You think you are supposed to break up with your current boyfriend, but you hate being single, and you work from home. Where will you meet people?

Fear uses the past to make you doubt where your intuition is leading you. You have a choice. Do you want to make decisions based on past limitations, or future freedom?

Challenge: For one hour today, listen to your intuition without judgment. When you pick a dinner spot with a friend or partner, don't check reviews, listen to your intuition. When you say yes to a date, don't ask your friends for advice. Make your own decision. Take a one hour siesta from questioning yourself. Start small. If you doubt yourself, no judgment. You will soon find that the "inconvenient" turns you take might not be mistakes, but much-needed detours.

Once you can go easy on yourself for having doubts, and all the strange places your intuition takes you, you can hear doubt's message.

Plug Into Doubt's Message: What Is The Right Choice?

Doubt told Alanna to stay with her boyfriend, even though she felt dissatisfied. She couldn't predict that months later she would meet someone that put her doubt to rest.

If I had known Alanna earlier, I would have suggested she acknowledge doubt's concerns: "Yes doubt, being single sucks sometimes. Yes doubt, all my friends are getting married. Yes doubt, my baby-making gap is closing." Does she have to spend energy avoiding each concern? No. She simply has to listen, glean any knowledge, and then keep moving toward what she wants.

The message behind doubt is to keep you rational and realistic.

Doubt is your cautious, blunt and analytical friend. Her logic is useful when it comes to planning a trip and setting goals. She helps you avoid mistakes and prepare for obstacles. When you get starry-eyed, doubt pulls you back to reality. While doubt is useful in some scenarios, she is not useful when she makes you settle.

Merriam-Webster Dictionary defines doubt as, "to believe that something is unlikely and to have no confidence in something or someone." Just because doubt exists to point out the unlikelihood, doesn't mean you have to live by her pessimism.

When doubt pipes up, listen. Suppressing her will only make her louder at inopportune moments. Doubt says there aren't any good men. Good to know. Doubt says that you should stay with your underwhelming partner because he is better than the last guy. Okay. Do you want to stop dating, or settle because of her thoughts? No. Sometimes she will help you avoid a major disaster. Other times, she will want to take the steering wheel and you will have to assertively put her back in the passenger seat. You get to choose what to do with her directions.

Get Honest

When Shauna sat down in my office, she was afraid that her husband was going to leave her. Contrary to what you might think, her husband hadn't done anything. No matter how many times she reminded herself of this, she didn't trust him. She knew she had trust issues. She didn't know that the person she distrusted the most was herself. I asked Shauna what I ask all clients experiencing trust issues.

Me: Do you doubt yourself?

Shauna: What do you mean? All men get bored, and he'll start looking over my shoulder any day now. I know he is different, but I just don't trust him.

Me: If that does happen, if he does leave you, do you trust that you will be okay?

Shauna: I've always been afraid that one day I'd end up alone. I watched my dad leave my mom." She thought for a moment, "He ended up fine. He married some 30 something, and she ended up raising me alone. I guess I've kept that image in my head since I was a kid.

Me: What makes you doubt that your husband will be different than your dad?

She had to think about that one. She couldn't answer until we worked through some deep seated doubts about men and anger toward her father's actions.

Shauna: My mom was a strong woman. She always said that God only gives us what we can handle. I guess I always worried that since I am strong, I'd have a hard life… things wouldn't come as easily for me.

Monsters Under The Bed

When you get honest, you uncover that beneath all doubt is self-doubt. Self-doubt makes surface doubt scary because you don't trust that you can handle what comes your way. Shauna didn't consciously think God was out to send her painful situations, but her past and her mom's words made her future look bleak.

Doubt is like a fretful child who reminds you about the monsters under the bed. You are the responsible parent who must lift up the bed curtain to put the fears to rest. The problem is that most women don't trust themselves enough to face the monsters.

RELEASE DOUBT EXERCISE

Take a moment to get honest about the doubts beneath your relational bed. Read the following trigger words to get the juices flowing.

Trigger Words:

I really really want... but that is just not realistic.

I'm afraid I'll have to settle for...

I always wanted... but it doesn't seem possible.

1. What do you fear/doubt might happen in your relationship?
2. In what ways do you doubt yourself?
3. In what ways do you doubt friends, family, higher powers to support you?

Take It Deeper

You can't predict what happens, but when you trust yourself, you can predict who you will be no matter what unpredictable situations arise in your relationship.

When did you learn to doubt yourself? Did you make choices in the past? Did other people teach you to doubt yourself? When was trust lost in yourself, others, and the divine? Jot down experiences and commit to bringing them to light with a trusted friend or practitioner.

When you voice your doubts, they lost their power. The disbelief doubt throws your way won't phase you because you trust yourself. You will trust your higher power. And, in the rare chance that doubt's forecast is accurate, you will trust yourself to be strong, brave and protected no matter what happens.

Remember Your Intention

Think of your intuition as an unused leg muscle. You go on a hike, only to get tired halfway up the mountain. Does your fatigue mean you were wrong to plan such a big hike or does it mean you have some leg workouts to do? When you are facing a doubt-inducing obstacle, and you want to give up, remember your intention. Your intention is it trust that reaching the mountain top is possible. You just need to practice self-trust workouts before you reach it.

When in doubt, you have lost trust.

The intention behind doubt is to trust, and to regain trust in yourself or your future.

While the ego finds trust through self-protection and certainty, your true self wants to regain trust by deepening your connection to your intuition or inner compass.

When I say intuition, I don't mean some new-age spidey-sense about what to do next. Intuition is not a psychic power, and it is definitely not your feelings. Intuition is your voice, when all apology, justification, shame, and people pleasing is removed. Intuition is your most authentic self, stripped clean of the costume of anyone else's opinions. The best way to reconnect with this authentic self, or intuition, is to reconnect with your inner child.

AN HONEST INNER CHILD EXERCISE

Close your eyes. See yourself as a five-year-old. Connect to what she wants in a relationship. Ask her the following questions:

1. What is your ideal partner like?
2. How does he treat you?
3. How will he make you feel?

When you ask a child about what they want, they don't limit themselves with rationale. Keep asking her what she wants. Notice how her answers are different than how you would answer. The differences stem from fear. Anytime you feel a limitation just exhale it back to where it came. She won't wonder if her request is too big. She won't worry about sounding greedy, or selfish or disillusioned. Kids trust that the images etched in their heart are there for a reason.

Your initial urge will be to think of every reason why your inner child's request is naive and unrealistic. When this hamster wheel starts turning, breathe. Then, choose to talk to your intuition as if it were the child you love. If your younger self asked you for this, how would you respond? Would you say, "Oh, sorry sweety, but all the good men are taken. I'll find you someone more realistic." Hopefully not. Your job is not to belittle or rationalize with your inner child. Your job is to listen to her deepest desires, and do your best to honor her with your actions.

Act On Your Intention

Imagine what the world would look like if everyone acted on the desires of their most authentic self. How would people treat each other? What relationships would they create? What families would they make? What norms would they pass down to future generations? Trusting your deepest desires is not selfish because it creates a gift for the generations relying on you to pave the way.

Now that you know your intentions aka your inner child's desires, you can let them shape your response to your current doubt-inducing situation. Take a look at the impact of acting with intention instead of reacting with doubt.

Imagine that you doubt that there is someone better than your current partner. You stays with him, only to get divorced in three years. Your kids have to schlepp back and forth between houses. They only see their dad every other weekend.

Then imagine that you have the same doubts, but your inner child desires a relationship that makes you feel inspired. Your partner is far from inspiring. He makes you feel like your career goals are a cute hobby. You trust yourself enough to leave him. Your are single for a year and have the freedom to travel, where you fall in love with volunteering. When you return to the states, you restructure your business to include social causes. In the midst of your business ventures, you meet a marketing expert. He invests in you, personally and professionally, if you know what I mean. Which scenario sounds more fun?

Although trusting your intuition and acting with intention sounds like a no-brainer, three fears may stop you.

Fear #1: Following my intuition feels scary.

Your intuition *will* want you to do something scary. Culture has concocted the fantasy that following your intuition feels peaceful. I've learned that following your heart rarely feels peaceful, but it always brings peace. Embrace the scares, feel the doubt and keep moving toward the freedom you deserve.

Fear #2: What if I fail?

Trusting your intuition requires a leap of faith. A leap of faith doesn't always lead to success. Sometimes a leap leads to falling thirty feet, which is exactly the place you need to be to start your new journey. Sometimes the future needs you to trust it before it shows you the finish line.

Fear #3: Following my intuition, instead of logic, is irresponsible
When your brain tells you that your heart's desires are irresponsible, remind it of its limited perspective, literally. Research shows that the heart is magnetically 5,000 times stronger and electrically 10,000 times stronger than your brain. Remember the inner child exercise, and take responsible action on her behalf.

Make a decision right now that for one entire day, even one hour, you will decide to trust yourself. Don't take any action unless you are checking in with your intuition. If you can't tell the difference between fear and intuition, reconnect to your inner child and ask her what she would do in this moment. While her requests won't always feel peaceful, they will always lead you to feel freedom.

Develop Your Skills

Doubt shows up to warn you that what your inner child wants might not be possible. Honor how doubt keeps you informed. Then, move doubt into the light. Ask if its warnings are leading to settling or safety.

In the light, doubt is the emotion of the spiritually intelligent. I guarantee that if you struggle with doubt, you value rationale and logic as much as you do humility and generosity. You never ask for more than what you think you deserve, but you also believe in limitless possibility.

When you respond to your obstacle with doubt's rational skill set, you can stay prepared while also fulfilling your desires. Sometimes, doubt arises to point out something you missed. Let your doubts balance your creative optimism with logic. Balance entails taking informed risks and not worrying about feeling disappointed if expectations fall through. The healthy "doubter" will trust that unmet expectations are where miracles happen.

What situation causes you doubt in your relationship? Make a list of what you know to be true, and what you don't know to be true about this situation. Declare the following truths:

Despite my doubts,
I trust that I will act...
I trust that I will be...
I trust that I am...
I trust that my higher powers will...

You don't feel doubt so you can worry and settle. You feel her so you can move toward your truth informed, aware, and equipped with clarity and caution. If you have doubts about the future, you will need courage to keep moving.

Enjoy The Saving Grace: Courage

The word courage comes from the word heart. When you begin to doubt, focus on a person you love. Focus on the inner child, future daughters, or the partner that lives in your heart, and follow your deepest desire for their sake. Focusing on someone you love will give you the courage you need to keep moving. Doing so will ease doubts since her saving grace is courage.

When you begin to doubt yourself or your future, ask: What is doubt warning me will happen? Is there anything I can do to protect myself from those warnings? Do I trust myself no matter what happens? Even if I don't, am willing to keep fighting on the behalf of those I love?

Your ego will make it difficult to answer these questions. Conditioned to need tangible evidence, your ego will make you skeptical. Your ego won't want you to move forward until you can prove that things will work out. When she demands proof, prepare yourself:

Evidence your ego looks to before it is willing to trust:

Similar experiences in the past

Advice from mentors

Logic

Probabilities

The realities playing out in friends' lives

Evidence that what you want is already happening

When you remain courageous despite a lack of the above, your ego will tempt to pull you back into your comfort zone, settling. She will want logic, or friends, or the past to confirm your faith in a better future. In these moments, use your saving grace. Courage will help you keep fighting for your inner child's desires despite the ego's hesitancy.

For example, a woman is single and doubts if she will find someone she truly loves.

Conditioned Response: I am going to give my ex a chance. He can't be that bad. I mean, other girls would kill to be with him. I might never meet someone else.

Upgraded Response: It might not seem logical, but I am going to hold out for the right guy. I don't need to date him when I know he isn't for me. I have a desire for a relationship for a reason. Despite what my friends say, I know I won't be disappointed.

Roadblocks On The Route To Trust

You will be afraid of getting too hopeful or excited: Overwhelming doubt sometimes stems from a childhood that taught you that trusting too much could lead to disappointment. You may have made a vow as a kid to never get excited because then you would look like an idiot if it didn't work out. If you face this obstacle, have the courage to break the vow, to get excited, and to get even more excited if something unexpected happens.

You will get impatient: You will get impatient and date someone who doesn't meet your needs. Don't enslave yourself to someone unworthy of you. A slave stays captive for three reasons: safety, fear or respect. If you are dating someone to stay safe from the dangers of loneliness, free yourself. If you are dating someone because you fear they are the best you can get, free yourself. If you are dating someone because you respect them and love them, then you are already free. Have the courage to patiently wait for a man that frees you.

Friends will say your standards are too high: If you break up with a boyfriend because you believe there is someone better, your family and friends will tell you it was a mistake. You will lose trust in yourself. You will feel doubtful. Have the courage to listen to your heart, even when others don't believe it. Their hesitation comes from their own fear and doubt.

Time will tick on...on...on: It is easy to trust when you keep getting validation from the universe. It is easy to stay optimistic when everything goes as planned. It is not so easy to stay hopeful when you have done everything you can think to do and nothing changes. When you start to doubt, have the courage to trust in unseen validation.

Your memory will work against you: If you tend to doubt yourself, your memory will enjoy showing you every memory where you trusted yourself only to be disappointed. Your brain will make you feel disillusioned, which will make you doubt yourself more. Have the courage to stop defining yourself based on the past.

You don't need to have all the answers; you can just courageously head toward where you know you must go. When doubt flares, use it to stay grounded in reality. Instead of being pessimistic, you can be the realist that your future relationship needs as it matures.

Make a commitment to how you want to use your logic within your relationship.

Can I Trust Too Much?

I just spent the entire chapter telling you to trust yourself and your higher power. I asked you to suspend limitation and believe in the impossible. Now, I will suggest the opposite. Like all life, your relationship landscape needs balance. In the next chapter, you will learn how empathy can make you trust *too much* in a partner that doesn't even trust himself. You will learn how to balance your ability to see his potential in a way that might surprise you.

6

Empathy: He Just Has So Much Potential

Empathy should never make you justify his bad behavior, but inspire you to respect yourself enough to let him go.

He could be so great if he just started pursuing something he loved. He could be so great if he just started caring more about his career. He could be so great if he had different friends, if he treated me better, if he could just stop being anything like how he currently is right now. Oh, empathy, you make us see the best in our men, even when our men are blind to it.

Empathy is handed to us without directions. When we misuse empathy, we date an idea of a man instead of the man himself. We see his potential instead of his choices, and we date that potential even when he doesn't see it for himself. Empathy was never meant to make us settle for potential.

EMPATHY IN DARK	EMPATHY IN LIGHT
Excuses abusive or destructive behavior	Has compassion, but holds partner accountable
Forgives partner, and stays in cycle of abuse for the purpose of helping the partner	Forgives partner for abuse, but respects self enough to leave cycle of abuse
Stays with partner because of partner's potential	Encourages partner's best, without banking on it
Waits for what partner *could be* instead of being honest about reality	Honors partner for what partner could be, but makes choices based on reality
Worries about hurting partner's feelings at expense of personal feelings	Navigates personal needs without worrying about hurting partner's feelings
Attracts narcissists and emotional leeches due to misused empathy	Sets boundaries that respect partner and self
Stays with wrong partner to avoid hurting partner's feelings	Focuses on partner's long-term good instead of the short term pain "leaving" will create

You must pair empathy with respect if you want to capitalize on the true intentions of this feminine superpower. By the end of this chapter, you will understand the difference between what you see in your partner versus what he sees in himself. You will be able to set boundaries, let go of what could be and accept what is, and you will be able to respect his goals for his life, even if they don't match yours.

Unplug Judgment

As I mentioned, I have a knack for dating cheaters. What was worse than the moment I found out, was the moment I took him back. I took him back, even though he slept with someone else, even though he lied, even though I knew better. I thought I had standards for Christ's sake. Why did I take him back?

If you had asked me then, I would have responded, "I understood why he did it. I can empathize with him. He must be going through so much pain to have done that. He didn't mean it. He feels so bad about it." Empathy drove me to lower my standards, and man did I judge myself.

When Empathy Becomes An Achilles Heel

When working with highly empathetic women, I watch for three scenarios that cause self-judgment. As you read each, filter the situations through your own life. Notice the difference between how empathy made you feel versus what empathy caused you to do in the situation.

I tried to fix him: In what ways did you try to fix your partner? Did you ever blame yourself for not fixing him? Did he end up with someone else who did seem to change him? How did that make you feel?

I stayed with him when I knew it wasn't working: When did you know he wasn't right? How long after that moment did you stay together? Do you hold any judgments about that?

I let him get away with abusive behavior: Abuse is any word, action or inaction that bruises. Did you let it slide when he nitpicked? Did you pretend you didn't care when he checked out other women? Did you condone any other destructive behaviors? Did you ever make excuses for him? What behaviors do you tend to justify?

While empathy might seem like an Achilles heel, believe me, it is your greatest gift. To avoid letting self-judgment shut you down, use prayer, meditation or tapping as you reflect on your answers. Then, empathize with yourself for the ways you've empathized with others. Only through self-acceptance can you to change the patterns that made you settle in the past. Acceptance allows you to receive empathy's higher message, a message empowered by high standards and thick boundaries.

Plug Into Empathy's Message: What Is Real Potential?

This is what I hear: He is literally everything I want except he isn't affectionate toward me… Except he nitpicks me, except he still texts his ex-girlfriend, except he cheated on me. But I totally understand why he did that. He had a really detached dad growing up so I understand why he is like this.

Empathy is the ability to understand and share the feelings of others. In relationships, empathy arises with a few messages. Unfortunately we respond to her inappropriately. As you read, notice when and where you feel empathy most often and how you respond to empathy.

Empathy helps you see from your partner's perspective: Don't use your empathetic perspective to justify his bad behavior. Use it to stop taking his actions personally. Ask: Why is he doing this? Most often, you will realize that his actions have nothing to do with you. Out of respect for yourself, and him, don't excuse abuse.

Empathy helps you justify his actions: You can easily see his motivations and intentions. Great. Empathy says, "I know that hurt, but this has nothing to do with you. He cheated, lied, manipulated because of the fear in his own mind, not because you deserved it." Instead of taking responsibility for his actions, respect him enough to let him face his own repercussions.

Empathy helps you protect his feelings: Empathy doesn't want you to protect his feelings at the expense of your own. Show yourself as much empathy as you show him. Ask: How would you want to be treated in this situation? Would you want to be pitied? Would you want to be held accountable? Treat him the way you want to be treated. The best way to protect his feelings is to release him to someone who loves him for who he is right now.

Empathy helps you see his highest potential: Seeing his potential allows you to encourage him toward it… if he wants to go there. Who is he created to be? Does he see that? Does he want to be that? Will I be content if he stays exactly how he is now? You can't coach someone toward a goal they don't want to reach. Empathy can show you his potential, and if he wants to reach it. Respect his decision.

Empathy, combined with fear and scarcity, makes you try to mold your partner into what you want, even when he doesn't want the same thing. When you are with a real man, he will want you to encourage him toward his potential, and to call him out when he lives less. Empathy, combined with love and respect, will help your partner grow.

I love my husband. I can see his potential, but that doesn't mean I need him to reach that potential in order for me to be happy. He could stay exactly how he is today and I would feel content. When he says something hurtful, I can see that his words come from his own fears and insecurities. I can forgive him without taking his actions personally, but I don't lie about how his actions affect me. As a man, he wants to be held accountable.

Empathy exists so you can forgive, love , and respect your partner, not so you can stay with a man that doesn't love, forgive or respect you, let alone himself.

Get Honest

Why do women buy fixer-uppers that don't want to be fixed? Mini science lesson: Humans have a deep investment in scarcity. Humans are wired to think there is not enough so they hold on to what they have.

The result: You might feel tempted to cling to what is in front of you, even if he leaves you feeling lack.

If you keep cycling back to men who *need* your empathy and forgiveness because they are far from what you want, it is time to get honest.

How Much Compromise Is Too Much?

Getting honest reveals the scarcity mindset that keeps you from owning the relationship you want. In the next exercise, you will uproot feelings of scarcity by getting honest about your partner's potential. If you are single, imagine a partner from the past.

THE 'COULD BE' EXERCISE

Recall a partner who "could be" so great, if only he changed a few things. With him in mind, complete the sentences. Notice if your answers are stressing you out. Are your shoulders hiked up to your ears? Is your jaw clenched? Do yourself a favor, and tap the stress reducing pressure points from in Chapter 02. After you calm your nervous system, record insights.

He could be so great if…
I just wish he would stop…
But I understand why because…
I am invested in him changing because…
I want him to change because I'm afraid that…
If I can't change him, that means…
If some other girl changes him that will make me feel…

If you can see his best, are you responsible for fixing and coaching him toward that best? No. Fear will tell you that he is the best you will ever get, so stay with him and fix him up. Scarcity is a lie, so don't let it make you desperate.

Just because you see potential in him doesn't mean you are obligated to coach him into a hypothetical highest potential. There are 7.6 billion people on the planet. There are plenty of non-imaginary men waiting to exceed your expectations. By staying with him, he might miss out on being met with open arms by one of the billions of women on the planet who have different expectations and standards than you.

The truth is, everyone has potential. That doesn't mean they get to put a ring on your finger.

Ask yourself: If someone showed me an image of the perfect partner for me, would I still be with this man? If the answer is no, you need to respect yourself, him, and his future partner and end the relationship. You can only receive your person when you are willing to get honest and let go of the wrong guys.

Remember Your Intention

In an interview with Oprah, Rihanna shared the story of when Chris Brown abused her.

Oprah asked Rihanna how she felt after Brown's abuse was released to the public. Rihanna broke down crying, not for the reason you imagine: "I felt protective. I felt like the only person they hit right now was him… because as angry as I was, as angry and hurt and betrayed, I just felt like he made that mistake because he needed help… and who's going to help him? Nobody's going to say he needs help. Everybody's going to say he's a monster without looking at the source. I was more concerned with him." Rhianna, a powerfully empathetic artist, had just been abused. Her response? She cried for Chris Brown.

I can't judge her. I've done the same thing. Instead of excusing herself from the bruises of his actions, Rihanna excused his abuse. Why did she feel empathy? She understood why he hit her. She felt his pain.

She took responsibility for protecting him. She saw why he hurt her, and she let that justify subjecting herself to further abuse. Been there, done that.

The truth is that Rihanna's empathy was leading her down a path that thousands of women have paved: You see your partner's best and excuse everything he does that falls short. If you are currently with someone who acts in ways you have to justify or excuse, it might be time to reclaim the true intention of your empathic feelings toward him.

The intention behind empathy is to see your partner's best and to relate to his feelings. But, wait! Just because you can see his potential, doesn't mean you need to fix him, change him, or wait around as he figures out how to get there.

HIS POTENTIAL VS. YOUR PATIENCE EXERCISE

What are you waiting to see a change in your partner?

What potential are you hoping he reaches?

What would change in your relationship if he reached this potential?

How long are you willing to wait for each change?

Are you waiting for him to be more caring? More motivated? More committed? Are you willing to wait until death do you part for this change to happen? No one is perfect, and grace is a huge part of a healthy relationship, but you need to be clear about what requirements you have for happiness. If you can't be happy until he changes, you might be due for a hard conversation. Your job is to love your partner where he is and to leave his changes up to him.

Empathy doesn't just want you to see his best. Empathy wants you to look within and honor your best. If a man constantly leaves you feeling drained, belittled, or broken, you need to empathize with yourself the way you would empathize with him. Honor the potential you see in him while honoring the reality of how his current choices make you feel.

Act On Your Intention

Rachel and her partner had broken up twice. They were giving their love one last go when she came to me. Apparently, her partner ridiculed her body. She forgave him. He told her that she wasn't his type. She forgave him. He made fun of her mannerisms, and not in a cute way. She forgave him. She wanted to get married, and he wasn't sure. She let that slide. Her fear kept her chained to a man that didn't even know if he wanted her. Fear, mixed with her empathy, was telling her to keep trying. Unfortunately, he wasn't telling himself the same.

When you act on empathy instead of listening to it, you take pity on your partner, which will either unintentionally condone his abuse or perpetuate a mentor-coach relationship. The intention of empathy is not to stay in a relationship where two people feel like they are not enough for each other.

In our first session, Rachel and I worked through her predicament. She could see how amazing he could be, but his efforts were anything but amazing. She believed in his best, and she knew how happy she would be if he changed. The reality is that he wasn't changing. Continuing to act on her empathetic wishes left her drained and desperate.

I urged her to act on her intentions: to honor his best, and to help him reach it. To do so, she needed to answer a tough question: What will motivate him to reach his potential? Staying with him or leaving him?

She had to leave him. He needed her to set higher expectations and to not coddle him. He needed her to stick up for herself. He needed her to set a boundary. She didn't end the relationship out of anger or blame. She ended it out of respect not only for herself, but for the man she knew he would be one day.

If your partner constantly falls short, you might need to answer the tough question. Do I stay or do I go? Which answer will honor the man you know him to be? When you act on your intention to see his best, while not taking responsibility for getting him there, you revolutionize your relational beginnings and endings. You know how to see his potential while loving him where he is. If you can't love him where he is, you have the courage to leave. In the next exercise, you will imagine both options: the option to stay, and the option to go.

A LETTER TO YOUR FUTURE DAUGHTER EXERCISE

Take one minute to free write about how you feel and think around your partner:

1. How does your partner make you feel on an average day?
    ie. He makes me feel insecure, small, frustrated, loved, seen, heard etc.
2. Make a list of what you need to see change in order for your relationship to work.
3. Go through your list and put a check next to any criteria that he will change in the next month. If he isn't changing in a month, he probably won't change in a year.
4. Pretend you have a daughter. She is 18 years old and she is in the exact relationship you are in right now. She just sent you a letter about how she feels in her relationship, how he makes her feel, what he isn't doing, and what he is doing to change. Now, use those empathy skills and write her back. What advice would you give her? What would you suggest she do?
5. If you took your own advice, what step might you take today?

It is important to write to a daughter that is 18, and not 30 because an 18-year old doesn't have the pressure of time. As my clients get older and pass the big 3-0, fear tells them that their eggs are dwindling and they need to find a husband. When you write to your daughter, you remember your intentions for yourself. You remember that your partner deserves to be with someone who doesn't need him to change. You remember that you deserve to be with someone who knows how lucky he is to be with you. Once you advise her, take one step toward your own advice.

Develop Your Skills

As you know, empathy lets you see his best, understand his motivations, give grace and encourage and motivate him toward his goals. Depending on how you use these skills, you can create either a healthy or a codependent relationship. Below are my best tips to develop your empathy muscle in a healthy way.

Differentiate between his best and your best: Yes he could be so great, but does he see that? Does he want that? Is he happy staying exactly the way he is right now? Don't judge him for not striving to change. Empathize, understand him, and decide if you want to be with him.

Let his actions speak louder than his words: Don't let a man tell you he will change. Let him show you. A good trick is to look at who he was one month ago or one year ago. Is he the same or different? You can love what he wants to become, but don't confuse that with loving him for who you think he *should* become.

Learn the art of repercussions: When you make excuses or justify his unconscious and hurtful behavior, you give him permission to stay in destructive patterns. Forgiveness doesn't have to condone behavior. There should be repercussions he can see or else he is coddled out of an opportunity to grow.

Learn the difference between what he says he wants, and what he needs: Your partner probably wants to make you happy. He probably loves you. He probably says he will change and that he wants to change. The truth is that your partner doesn't want to constantly feel inadequate because you want and need more from him. He needs to be loved for who he is right now. If you can't love him now, you need to let him go.

Live in the present: It is easy to let empathetic feelings justify his actions. "He cheated because he has jealousy issues. He has commitment issues because his parents had a toxic relationship. He is critical of me because he is so critical of himself." You don't need to excuse his present behavior just because there are excuses in his past. Staying with him after he has belittled you, cheated on you, or disrespected you, gives him permission to do whatever he wants as long as he can provide a reason. Let his present actions speak louder than his past excuses.

Talk to yourself the way you would a friend: You probably show more empathy to your partner and friends than to yourself. Find balance. What would you say to a friend in this situation? Would you say, "I know he slept with your best friend, but he had a really rough childhood. Cut him some slack"? Hmm. Or would you say, "You deserve better. Let him go"? Talk to yourself as if you empathized with your own feelings.

Develop your empathy by doing what you do best, giving advice. What would you tell a friend or daughter in the same situation? Whatever question you face, whatever conflict arises, give yourself your own empathic and wise advice.

Enjoy Your Saving Grace: Respect

When you close this book, you might find yourself tempted to fall back into old codependent patterns. You might date an idea of a man because you feel responsible for changing him. You might attract a partner who falls short because he senses you excuse and empathize with his inexcusable behavior. When you find yourself in old unhealthy patterns, employ empathy's saving grace: respect.

Imagine that your partner does that thing he said he would never do. He begs for forgiveness for the twelfth time. What response is most respectful for you and him? If your friend or daughter were experiencing this, what advice would you give?

Conditioned Response: You justify in your mind what he did, recalling the hard childhood he had. You say, "I understand baby. It's okay that you did that." Subconsciously this sends the message that there are no repercussions for his actions.

Upgraded Response: I understand why you did that, but out of respect for myself and the man I know you want to be, I can't be with you when you treat me that way.

You better believe that when you suddenly respect yourself enough to stop taking someone's abuse, they will push back. The women I work with know that when they leave my office, they will be tempted to fall back into old excuses. To prep them, I warn them of four temptations where they can practice combining empathy with respect.

Roadblocks On The Route To Respect

You will worry about hurting his feelings: Respect him enough to not pity him. He might want you to coddle him, but his higher self wants you to trust that he is a big boy who can handle life without you. If you decide to end the relationship and worry about upsetting him, keep this in mind: What hurts more? Breaking up now? Or egging him on for six more months and then ending it? Rip off the band-aid before the glue grows stronger.

He will make you feel guilty for not trusting him: Especially in the case of cheating or abuse, your partner might use guilt tactics to get you to forgive him. "I didn't mean it. Please forgive me. You have to trust me. It didn't mean anything. I wish I could take it back baby." When a partner pushes you to trust him, tell him that trust and forgiveness are not the same. Forgiveness is a choice. Trust is earned. If he has shown you an untrustworthy version of himself for months, you deserve at least an equal number of months for him to show you otherwise.

He will show signs of improving: Respect yourself enough to know that you deserve more than, "signs of improving." He deserves more than to constantly feel inadequate despite his improvements. You deserve more than a partner who barely reaches your expectations. You deserve a man who blows your expectations. Respect him and his future partner enough to set him free.

He will have a major life crisis: It's true. As soon as you decide to leave him, he will have a life crisis. Something will happen that makes your empathy buttons flare. He will lose his job. His parent will get sick. His dog will pass away. In these scenarios, you will feel the need to stay and care for him. To avoid this codependent tendency, respect what he is going through by weaning him off of you. Weaning him off of your loving care, challenges him to find support from ready and willing family, friends and future partners.

Relationship therapists share the same message. Man's greatest need is to be respected. You can respect your partner enough to not coddle his bad behavior, or nitpick his inadequacies. Women's greatest need is to be loved. You can love yourself enough to take your own advice and walk away from destructive, unloving relationships.

You are not wired with empathy to see your partner's best and to fix him. You feel empathy so you can see who your partner will become, and decide if you want to be there if and when he changes.

Changing The Past

Speaking of wanting to change something about someone, have you ever wished you could change something about yourself? When you are single, you have spare time to reflect on past choices. Dare I say, reflection leads to shame and regret about "bad" choices. Don't let shame-inducing thoughts put you in a spiral of self-deprecating singleness. While it sounds counter-intuitive, shame and regret don't have to steal your peace. In the next chapter, you will learn to use moments you regret to reach a new level of wholeness in your relationship.

PART THREE

Single

*"Her best beauty trick is remembering where she comes from
and not apologizing for where she is going."*
– Danielle Bennett

7

Shame: I Feel Like a Fool for Dating Him

♥ ♥ ♥

*Shame is not an excuse to beat yourself up, but an opportunity
to stop defining yourself by your worst moments.*

How could I have fallen for him? What was I thinking? That was so embarrassing! I can't believe I dated him, but I did. The worst part of dating the wrong guy is not the months or years spent with him, but the shame that is left when you finally leave.

Erica was taking a year off men. She hoped 365 days of solitude would deactivate the magnets that drew narcissists in like metal fragments. Inevitably, a seemingly humble man, keyword 'seeming', convinced her to go on a date. After three months too long, she realized that she had wound up with yet another egomaniac. By that third month, he was showing all the signs of a full-blown narcissist:

making her feel guilty for his actions, condescending her for her unique viewpoints, blaming all conflict on her, and expecting her to drop everything to support his career goals. Meanwhile, he had zero interest in what she did for a living. She had books on this stuff. How did he slip through her discerning filter?

Imagine that Erica had an alter ego. Imagine that this other version didn't shame herself for her past. Instead, she explored why she felt ashamed. She felt ashamed because she didn't like making 'stupid' decisions. In all honesty, she liked making perfect decisions, all of the time, and not showing herself grace when she slipped. Ah, good to know. Instead of beating herself up about her situation, she decided to not be the kind of girl who let her worst decisions define her.

Both women felt ashamed about who they dated. The first version let the choice define her. The second version left her choice in the past, so she could make new choices in the future. If you are regretting your toxic relationships, you can use them as an opportunity to reclaim your identity from choices that have no right defining you.

This chapter is for my ladies who have dated some real "winners." If you have been beating yourself up since the breakup, I'm here to say that the shame is showing up for a reason. I don't recommend repressing your regrets, but learning the art of responding to them in a more productive and upgraded way.

You might be in the habit of responding in a not-so upgraded way. You self-deprecate over past decisions you wish you could erase. If your partner asks, you edit your past. If he finds out the truth, you apologize for what you did. When you keep reacting with shame like this, you wind up attracting partners who mirror back to you your own feelings of inadequacy.

SHAME IN THE DARK	SHAME IN THE LIGHT
Apologetic	Honest, unapologetic and free
Overly timid	Sensitive and in touch with partner's feelings
Plays a victim card	Makes empowered choices
Covers up flaws	Opportunity to release beliefs that make you feel flawed
Defines you by worst moments	Reminds you to forgive yourself for "worst" moments
Convinces you to hide your authentic self	Reveals areas of embarrassment so you can be more authentic
Harbors guilt about the past	Reveals opportunity to separate past choices from current identity
Anticipates and expects rejection	Courageously embraces authenticity despite rejection
Judges yourself based on your "right" and "wrong" choices	Makes choices based on higher truth
Convinces you that past events are unforgivable	Reminds you to never let past actions define you
Attract partners who don't stand in their power	Attracts partners who powerfully embrace freedom and choice

You can embrace shame-inducing obstacles by allowing each to reveal limiting beliefs and areas of inadequacy. When you uncover areas of self-rejection, you unearth opportunities to heal and grow. You put an end to self-ridicule, and the relationships it manifests. By the end of the chapter, you will be able to connect to your inner rebel, who will empower you to stand up against limiting beliefs, "shameful" relationship patterns, and partners who define you by your worst moments.

Unplug Judgment

Like us all, Erica judged her dating "mistakes." The more she judged herself, the more she manifested moments she regretted. I am not saying she created the problem; I am saying that we accept the treatment that we give to ourselves. As she beat herself up daily, she was unconsciously inviting others to do the same. Her self-judgment trapped her in a very unpleasant cycle.

Erica's shame cycle: Beat herself up about her dating history > Hide her history from others > Feel like a fraud > Date men who reinforce her insecurities > Feel even more insecure > Feel incapable of changing her dating story > Feel even more ashamed.

Erica's upgraded cycle: Accept her dating history > Own (and even joke about) her dating choices > Feel honest and empowered when she shares her hard-earned wisdom > Separate her dating choices from her identity > Feel confident > Date men who reflect her confidence > Feel free to change her relationship story.

You Are Not Your Choices

When you stop judging yourself based on your regrets, you bring shame's self-esteem crushing voice into the light. Instead of hiding your regrets, where they undermine your life, you bring them into your conscious awareness. You go easy on yourself. You can even poke fun, because you are *not* your past. You are not your shame. You just feel ashamed, for a moment. As you read about how Erica stopped judging her past, filter her journey through your own experience.

She made three decisions that helped her accept her past choices. She didn't make these decisions with her head, but with her whole heart. If you need to employ prayer or mindfulness tools as move through the following exercise, go for it. As you read each decision, take a minute to pause and internalize the shifts.

Accept what you did. Acceptance doesn't mean that you would choose it again. Acceptance means that the past lives in the past, and the future can be different.

Close your eyes and imagine "shameful" memories as small marbles, like the memories in the movie Inside Out. Watch the memories grow smaller and smaller until they pale in comparison to your best memories.

Separate your choices from your identity. Yes, you are accountable for your past actions, but your actions don't have to determine who you are now. A little thing called grace exists. Your higher powers don't give you grace just so you can give it away to everyone but yourself. Write it on your mirror if you need to: Your choices don't define your truth. Your truth defines your choices.

Close your eyes again and imagine that every memory you have exists inside of you. See the memory marbles floating in your body, your stomach, your head or wherever else you feel them. Hold out your hand and let all the marbles fill your hand. Then release the marbles, into the ground or sky, or a guardian angel's hands. Look within. Notice that no matter how many moments you release, your true self still remains.

When you free your identity from past choices, your future choices are free to change.

Take the wisdom and leave the rest. If you do make a mistake, you might as well learn from it. What does your former self want to hear from you? Give her a pep talk and thank her for what the memories taught you.

Bring to mind an "unforgivable" moment from your dating history. See the moment on a movie screen. What is the theme of the movie? What does the main character (you) learn? How does the main character change? What does she know to never do again?

You can't change the past. You can only take notes and decide what choices you want to make in the future. Judgment does nothing but nail you to the cross of your past. You are not made to be a martyr. You are made to experience, to learn and to shine your wisdom on others.

Plug Into Shame's Message: What Have I Rejected in Myself?

Remember that text you sent to your ex-boyfriend, that guy you kissed after too many drinks, that photo you posted at 2 a.m.? While guilt makes you feel badly about what you did, shame makes you feel badly about who you are. Shame scours your memory for moments you regret and delivers them as sour pits in your stomach. You don't feel bad about what you did, but bad about yourself for doing it. Is shame trying to ruin your day? No.

For a minute, imagine that shame was a guardian angel. What if she had one job? To help you love yourself more. What if she reminded you of mistakes so that you could learn to love yourself despite them? What if she wasn't punishing you when she reminded you of past relationships? What if she pointed them out as an opportunity to stop letting them define you?

It is just a theory, but I believe that every time I feel shame, it is an opportunity for some much-needed self love. When you feel shame, recognize her positive message, "Hey, over here. Love this. Forgive that. That guy you dated? Let him go. That mistake you made? Don't let it define you. Let yourself off the hook."

The purpose of shame is to point out self-rejection so you can replace it with self-acceptance.

CHANGE YOUR STORY EXERCISE
Developed by holistic wellness practitioner Lynn Poinier.

As you answer each question, notice how you have the power to make meaning of your obstacles. You can let them be sources of shame, or you can change the story. You can focus on what you regret. Or, you can focus on your values and higher identity. Give it a try.

1. What relationship obstacle do you keep experiencing?
    Example 1: I always date narcissists
    Example 2: I go on one or two dates and then it ends
2. What is shameful about that obstacle (#1)?
    Example 1: I should have better discernment
    Example 2: I should be interesting enough to make men stick around
3. What is shameful about that (#2)?
    Example 1: I hate seeming stupid
    Example 2: I shouldn't think I am anything special
    Keep following the rabbit trail of shame until you find the root. You will know you hit the root when you get angry, or tears start leaking down your cheeks.
4. Why are these patterns shameful to you? What must you want?
    Example 1: I want to make responsible choices
    Example 2: I don't want to be arrogant; I want to care more about others
5. What kind of person wants #3? A person who values...
    Example 1: a person who values responsibility
    Example 2: a person who cares about others
6. Turn this value statement into an identity statement.
    Example 1: I am responsible
    Example 2: I care about others

Of course you feel ashamed about some choices. You have values! When you don't live up to those values, the natural reaction is shame. Instead of stifling the feeling, listen to her message. Listen to what you value. Then, honor yourself for having values. Just imagine someone who felt zero regrets, zero remorse, or zero desire to change the same situation you find yourself in today. Honor yourself for wanting to uphold your values.

When Erica fell for yet another narcissist, she felt ashamed. Up until our work together, she used her situation as proof that she was messed up. After she changed her story, she saw it as confirmation that she valued making smart choices. Good to know! Message received.

Your little shame angel is not punishing you. She is loving you, and calling you to love yourself and others more. The real beauty of embracing shame is that every ounce of love you give to yourself becomes love you can share with others.

Get Honest

Answer this relational riddle: Jane has a one night stand and feels ashamed about it. Her sister has a one night stand and does not feel ashamed about it. Who do you judge less? The ashamed sister feels more moral, right? If you get honest about your shame, you might find that you are holding onto it as a way to feel better about what you've done.

Self Punishment Doesn't Change The Past

Hannah had been traveling around the world, styling artists before they stepped on stage. She called me because she regretted leaving her kids at home while she worked. She had waited so long to deal with her feelings, that she had stopped enjoying her work. Instead of feeling and releasing the shame, she had been holding onto it. Some unconscious part of her felt that if she wasn't ashamed, she was a bad mother.

Most of my clients aren't ashamed about what they did or didn't do. They are ashamed of forgiving themselves given what they did. They are ashamed of loving themselves despite the imperfections. The irony is that withholding self-love only instigates more experiences that make it impossible to feel good about themselves.

FORBIDDEN TO FEEL GOOD EXERCISE

1. What do you feel ashamed about?
2. How is shame keeping you from feeling good about yourself?
3. What would happen if you felt good about yourself despite what happened?
4. What hesitation do you feel toward this?

Choose to get honest about your shame. Use your mindfulness techniques, and tap as you think through your answers. Then decide to love yourself anyway. Decide to be proud of who you are anyway.

Hannah kept shame around as self-punishment. It made her feel better about the ways she was falling short as a mom. Of course Hannah wasn't falling short. She just had ideas about what a mother should be, and she wasn't meeting those outdated expectations. When she was brutally honest about why she felt ashamed, she realized that carrying regret wasn't helping her parent well. Getting vulnerable about her regrets as a mom freed her to enjoy her work again and to appreciate her ability to be a role model for her kids.

If you struggle with shame, look to religious teachers as the anti-role model. Religion is famous for using shame to control behavior. Clearly shame-tactics don't work. The more shame someone feels, the more likely they are going to do it, just not in the open. If you want to start making healthier decisions, get honest about your shame-tactics. Get honest about if they are working. Then, get honest about what tactics will actually motivate you to make healthier choices.

Like a good teacher, you don't need to punish yourself for the past. You can set expectations, be honest about what you want, and encourage yourself to take action based on your higher intentions.

Remember Your Intention

Imagine that every time you looked in the mirror, you refused to enjoy your reflection until every imperfection was removed. Maybe you actually do this. Well, shame does this. Shame points out your imperfections, but not for the reason you might think. What if shame did exist to point out imperfections? What if she didn't want you to hide, judge, or regret your imperfections? What if she just wanted you to notice, accept, and learn to love yourself despite them?

The positive intention behind shame is self-acceptance and love.

Have you ever shared a part of your dating history with someone? Did you edit out the unattractive plot twists? Did you blur some key facts to appear a different way? Did you try to lipo aspects of your personality because someone told you they were ugly? Instead of focusing on the imperfect parts of your past, what if you focused on accepting yourself despite them? My best tool for regaining self-acceptance is to focus on your intention, instead of your regret.

FIND YOUR INTENTION EXERCISE

1. What parts of yourself and your past do you cover up?
2. Why is it difficult to accept or love yourself given each regret?
3. How do you wish you had acted?
4. Can you act this way now? Write your intentions below.

You might not use a mirror to cover imperfections, but you use your words, your titles, and your social media to hide the parts of yourself that you don't want others to see. When you feel ashamed, notice what you are hiding. Instead of hiding, honor the fact that you can even see your mistakes. Then, thank shame for reminding you to love yourself despite them.

Act On Your Intention

It takes ovaries to be who you are. Women who have less confidence and more shame will want to drag you to their level of self-shaming and ridicule. Don't let their shame dictate your life. The nicest thing to do for them is to be a beacon. Show women how you can value yourself despite the imperfections and mistakes in your past.

How would you act if you believed you were worthy of love?
How would you react to rejection?
How would you respond to critique?
How would you feel about "mistakes"?
How would your relationship look different?
How would you feel?
How would you act?

You might be in the habit of covering up your flaws. I mean, cover-up makes you more attractive, right? No. It is not your job to cover up aspects of yourself you don't like. It is not your job to harbor guilt about your mistakes. It is not your job to worry about what a man finds lovable and to edit accordingly. It is not your job to strive toward a love you already deserve. You don't need to be flawless to be lovable. When shame strikes, bring it on. Love who you are and act accordingly, despite this momentary emotion that tempts you to self-edit.

When you act on your intention to like yourself, instead of avoiding parts of yourself you don't like, everything changes. You are honest about your past because your worst moments don't define you. You don't take rejection, or praise, personally because others' opinions have nothing to do with you. You are proud of yourself and who you are becoming because stumbling is just part of the journey.

Make a decision, right now, that despite regrets, you will love yourself. Despite rejection, you will like the crap out of yourself. Despite friends and partners treating you like the old you, you will act according to the new you.

Develop Your Skills

I used to think that being "weird" was unattractive, so I blotted it out with my concealer. That made me attract guys who were into more "put-together" girls, guys who expected me to be something I wasn't. I can't blame them. I presented false expectations. I am not put together. I am messy and free and weird, and my husband loves it.

How do you feel your shame and let it transform your relationship?

You recognize that shame is the temptress. She tempts you to cover up your flaws. Once she determines what you should conceal, you have a choice. Do you obey her, or do you take her skill set to a new level?

Be Magnetically Authentic

If you cover up parts of yourself, you will attract men who aren't right for you. They won't appreciate your imperfections because you never revealed them. Once your quirks inevitably introduce themselves, you will feel even more ashamed if he reacts negatively. But wait. What if you use shame's habits in a healthier way? What if instead of concealing flaws, you concealed your need to be perfect? What if instead of hiding the imperfections you "shouldn't" have, you unapologetically flaunt them. Who knows, you might just attract a partner who loves your unapologetic and rebellious attitude.

Let's brainstorm ways you can use shame's two skill-sets for good: 1) "Should" thinking and 2) Covering up imperfections

1. **"Should" Thinking:** Should implies you know what is best. I should be like this. I shouldn't be like that. I should have known better. I

shouldn't have dated him. Whenever you say should, you are expressing deep-seated shame. How can you use "should" thinking to help your relationship?

Be proactive. If you know what you "should" do, then stop saying it and start choosing it. Emily and I made a deal that whenever she said "should", she would stop and make a choice. Notice how different "I should" versus "I choose" feels in your body.

I shouldn't have dated him vs. I choose to date a giving and caring person.

I should have known better vs. I choose to move more patiently.

I shouldn't talk so much vs. I choose to listen more.

I should have predicted he would be an ass vs. I choose to forgive myself for not being a fortune teller.

Choices put an end to shame-inducing patterns.

2. **Covering up**: Shame's second skill is a knack for covering up. While life taught you which parts of yourself to cover up, you can choose to cover up something new. The truth is that the only part of you worth covering up is the part of you that rejects yourself. From now on, cover up the voice in your head that tells you that you are flawed. Take an hour a day to fast from self-rejection. Carry a notebook, or use your phone. When you feel the urge to reject or shame yourself, grab a piece of paper and write it down. Then cross it out, delete it, and replace it with a proactive "I choose" statement.

Practice makes perfect, and you have tons of practice. Just pretend you are working for a new boss, and she wants you to put your skills to use in a more productive way. Have fun with this. The more fun you have, the more fun you will have owning your flaws with a partner who loves the unedited version of you. Speaking from experience, the traits you hide are the traits that your soul mate will find magnetic.

Enjoy Your Saving Grace: Rebellion

If you find yourself slipping into old patterns of self-ridicule and regret, use your saving grace: rebellion. Rebel against the urge to define yourself based on your past. You're a rebel for crying out loud. You're a natural at being yourself, despite any opinion, label or reputation.

A rebel is someone who does not conform to the expectations or patterns of others. Do not conform to what the past expects of you. Do not conform to what your ex-boyfriend expects of you. Do not conform to what fear expects of you. Shame tells you when and why you have rejected yourself, and then you get to rebel against that very same voice.

EMBRACE YOUR INNER REBEL EXERCISE

The next time you feel shame ask yourself:

What am I letting define my identity?
Is this identity true?
If not, how can I rebel against that identity?
How can I act on my truth instead of my shame?

Imagine that you date someone for three months. You trust him. You promise to not make the same mistakes again. Then, time reveals that he is even worse than the last guy.

Conditioned Response: How could I have wasted all that time!? I should have known better. I wish I had trusted myself from the beginning. I knew this would happen! I am so ashamed of myself.

Upgraded Response: Thanks shame. Apparently, I still reject myself for not dating the perfect people. This doesn't have to define me! I rebel against the habit of judging myself for this. I honor my intention to have high expectations. While it doesn't define me, it can inform me. I choose to be more discerning next time.

Inevitably you will find yourself scrolling through words, actions or inaction that you regret. Keep yourself from backsliding by exploring common challenges.

Roadblocks On The Route To Rebellion

Memories will arise that you regret: Don't let fear shove evidence of old versions of you into your face. Rebels don't let themselves be confined. Rebel against the past when it threatens to confine you.

Others will shame you: Your sweet family and past partners will treat you based on an obsolete version of yourself. Rebels don't care about others' opinions. Let them think what they want. If you are currently with someone, sit down with them. Hear them out. Apologize for ways that you have hurt them and then tell them how you are now making conscious choices to change.

Friends will judge you for jumping into a new relationship: Sometimes time off is beneficial. Other times, taking "a year off men" is rooted in the belief that there is something wrong with you, something that needs to be fixed. Your friends will try to shame you into not dating. Girl, you don't need to be fixed. If your motivation for taking a year off is to have fun and enjoy your last years of singlehood, do it. If your motivation is to fix yourself, then rebel against the belief that you are broken.

Collect evidence of other people who rebel well: Make a list of five people who have made similar "mistakes" or carry similar "imperfections", but who don't let those situations define them.

You were not given shame to flounder in self-rejection. The feeling invites you to face areas of self-rejection, so you can heal. When you recognize shame, thank her for guiding you closer to the unconditional love that will transform you, your partner, and your relationship.

Performance As An Identity Is Fatal

In the same way that your past does not define you, neither does your performance. When you find your worth in performance, perfection, appearance or opinion, you end up feeling insecure. It is especially easy to feel insecure when you are one of the only single ladies left in your friend group. In the next chapter, find out how insecurity is inviting you into a deeper level of confidence.

8

Insecurity: I Hate That
I Care What He Thinks

*Insecurity is not a sign of weakness, but an opportunity
to connect to your greatest source of strength.*

C andice checked her phone for the 120th time. No messages.
He said he wanted to hang out this week, but the week was
gone. Did she do something wrong? Did she say too much?
Was she too vulnerable? Was she too opinionated? The more red
marks she slashed through herself and the night, the more insecure
she felt.

When she didn't hear back from him, she went into self-preservation
mode. I don't like him anyway. I have other options anyway. I'm too
busy with my career anyway. If you feel for Candice, you've probably

had your fair share of insecure moments. Although self-preservation and self-editing are a typical response to insecurity, you don't have to be typical.

At its unhealthiest, insecurity will tempt you to take a man's opinion, his reactions, or his lack of action personally. You might start people pleasing, self-editing, and desperately seeking validation. Jealousy will creep in as you compare yourself to his ex, or to the girl across the table. Insecurity, in the end, is out to test your worth.

INSECURITY IN DARK	INSECURITY IN LIGHT
Second guesses yourself	Reveals opportunity to connect with worth and ground yourself in truth
Worries about partner's opinions	Respects the difference between partner's opinions versus personal opinions
Reverts to self-protection mode by closing off, avoiding vulnerability, and denying true feelings	Sets boundaries and approaches new relationships patiently
Edits true self in order to secure love	Shares true self so you can receive true love for the real you
Edits personality or opinions depending on partner's	Aware of different opinions and stands firm
Compares yourself to other women and ex-girlfriends	Recognizes and admires traits in other women that you wish to embody
Feels jealous	Respects beauty in others

At its healthiest, insecurity can remind you to never put your worth in unworthy places. She rises up to say, "Hey! Over here. Doesn't it feel gross to put your worth in his opinion? Okay, then stop." If you go out with a new date, you will be yourself, instead of being what he wants. If he doesn't call you back, you will call it a blessing, not a rejection. If he starts dating a beautiful woman, you will be able to compliment her instead of criticizing yourself. When you learn to respond to insecurity in a more productive way, you will reclaim your identity from unworthy sources.

Clients who come to me to work on confidence and insecurity issues tend to be my most compassionate and caring clients. They can see why everyone else is amazing, but have trouble turning that attitude inward. Let's upgrade your insecurity into its counterpart, honesty, so you can get honest about who you are, what you're worth and how you can add unique value to your relationships.

Unplug Judgment

Imagine a child that is blindfolded. What if I took that child and put them on the edge of a trampoline, facing the buoyant surface. The child feels stable, secure, and grounded until she steps forward and sinks into the movable surface. Is the child unstable? Of course not. The surface she stands on is to blame.

Misused insecurity makes women balance on the edge of a dating trampoline. My clients are independent, strong and empowered people. They feel frustrated when they get jealous and insecure around a guy. They want to feel grounded but find themselves moving from confidence to insecurity in a matter of seconds. In these moments, they feel insecure and unstable, but they are not. It is the foundation they walk on that is actually insecure.

Do you feel confident in one moment, but wildly insecure in the next? What changed? Have you ever felt self-assured in one relationship, and self-conscious in another? What was the difference? What opinions, validation or outcomes were you trying to stand on for security?

Why Do I Care What He Thinks?

When you start feeling insecure or jealous, be kind to yourself. It is not your fault that you have a habit of standing on insecure foundations. Everywhere you look, women are pressured to find their worth in opinions, professions and appearance. Let the following social studies lessons help you cut yourself some slack.

Thanks Culture: Culturally, women are taught to be nice little girls. You learn it is more important to curtsy to a man's desires than honor your own. While this cheery 18th-century mentality helped women's prospects in the era of marrying up, it now leaves you feeling insecure and inauthentic.

Thanks Fear: Fear will tell you that people won't like you unless you are perfect. Take 60 seconds to define perfect. I bet you can't. Your idea of perfect is usually a compilation of shoulds and shouldnts that are unrealistic and boring. I should be sweeter. I should be more agreeable. I shouldn't be so opinionated. I shouldn't make mistakes. I should look like a photo-shopped version of a bulimic woman. Mmm, no thank you.

Thanks Arranged Marriage: The next time you feel jealous, thank your sisters from the past. A few centuries ago, women relied on arranged marriage. Depending on their looks, their income, their status and their age, they had a better shot at getting hitched. These tendencies are in your DNA, but they are no longer relevant. You can be any type of woman, with any job, with any last name, of any age, and fall in love, or not. Comparing yourself to other women is no longer relevant or helpful.

Back in the day, a woman's survival depended on marriage. If she didn't find a suitable mate, she might not survive. Her only means of income, security or legacy was through a husband. People pleasing, hiding flaws and worrying about a potential partner's opinions were survival tactics. Oh, how times have changed.

You no longer need to people please, self-edit or self-protect to survive. Despite the DNA-etched urge to worship a man's opinion, you now have zero obligation to give a duck, (or that other word that rhymes). There is no reason to rely on a man's opinion, but if you catch yourself caring, don't beat yourself up. They are habits you never consciously chose. Now you know. In the meantime, insecurity is showing up for a reason. Listen up.

Plug Into Insecurity's Message: Where Am I Putting my Worth?

Confidence is the flakiest of states, leaving at the exact moment you need it most, on a first date, when you are ridiculed, or when you meet your partner's ex-girlfriend. Most people will tell you that insecurity means you need to be more confident. That advice is probably not helpful. The truth is, you are confident at home, with friends and at work. For some reason, your confidence flies out of sight when dating is thrown into the mix.

When Candice didn't hear back from her date, she could fall into old habits, comparing herself to his model ex-girlfriend and wasting hours stalking his social media photos. She could let insecurity take control, or she could acknowledge its message: "Hey, you are resting your worth on his opinion." It might have been easier to stifle the feeling with distractions, but listening was the first step in ending the habit.

Rebuild Shaky Foundations

Candice was finding her value in the ever-changing opinion of her date, instead of the eternal value she can only find within herself. Her insecurity showed up so she could reclaim her value. If you have felt insecure in the past week, you might be ready to hear this underlying message yourself.

Insecurity is a signal that you are finding your worth in an insecure source. Insecurity's positive message is that only you can define your worth.

If your source of security is unstable, your confidence will be unstable. The world will tell you that you need to change in order to be confident. Don't change, just change where you are standing.

When do you feel most insecure?

In this moment, where are you finding your worth?

What opinion, outcome, or validation is impacting you?

Is this a stable source? If yes, what actions can you take? If no, where do you want to find your worth?

You might feel insecure when you date someone with a mediocre job if you find your worth in status. You might feel insecure when a man rejects you if you rest your worth in someone's opinion. You might feel insecure if you gain weight if you rest your worth on appearance.

Get the idea? Notice when you feel insecure. Notice themes. Then you can be honest about where you find your worth, so you can rebuild a stronger foundation.

Get Honest

You already know who you are, the issue is that there is a very old tape recorder humming beneath your thoughts. You have to bring this tape recorder to the surface if you want to be free from its manipulative words. It tells you that you are not enough, and it is lying. Get real about your inner self-talk, so you can excommunicate unhelpful narratives from your inner dialogue.

OUT YOUR INTERNAL DIALOGUE EXERCISE

1. In your relationship history, when have you felt insecure?
2. Give the event a title: _____
3. On a scale of 0-10, how insecure do you feel when recalling this event? ____
4. In the moment, where were you resting your security? Read the common sources of security below and notice which resonate.
    Common Sources of Security:
    Comparison to another woman
    A man's opinion
    Validation
    A past version of myself
    Appearance
    Weight
    Social Status
    Success level
    Mood
5. Complete the following sentence starters:
    Man, I feel so insecure in this moment because…
    I have to care about his judgment because…
    I have to care about his opinion because…
    I have to compare myself to this other woman because…
    I learned to worship these sources of security when…

Notice how each sentence makes you feel. If the sentences make you feel intensely insecure, revisit each with your mindfulness tools. Keep breathing, meditating or tapping out of them until you reach a sense of clarity and calm.

Once you've regained a sense of confidence, reflect on your answers again. What did it feel like to say, I have to care about his opinion? Who taught you that you had to care? Jot down memories or insights as to where you learned each habit.

Who Do You Worship?

If you change who you are because of someone or something, you are worshipping them. The best way to snap out of a moment of insecurity is to frame your source of security as an object of worship.

Say it loud and clear:

I feel insecure because I am worshipping _____.

Examples: his opinion, his critique, a certain outcome, my looks etc.

I know you aren't consciously bowing down and kissing anyone's toes, so get honest, get conscious, and start worshipping a higher source.

This is not your first rodeo. You probably learned to care about opinions, validation and shallow foundations far before your dating years. Maybe you had a critical dad. Maybe you had a junior high crush who broke your heart. Maybe you had a beautiful sister. While it made sense to care back when you were a kid, your childhood habits are now hurting you.

The majority of your habits are formed before the age of ten. Recall a moment in your past when you placed confidence in an insecure source. Who in your family worshiped looks? Who made you treat success like a god? Who lived as if status was more important than integrity? Which parent modeled people pleasing to you? If manageable, repeat the OUT YOUR INTERNAL DIALOGUE EXERCISE from above with this early childhood event in mind. The earlier you go, the more change you will create. If the moment you recall feels intense or traumatic, pause and seek out support. You can contact me for a free phone consultation to process the moments that arise.

Your deepest insecurities are usually not your own. You learn to worship people's opinions, income and looks from unconscious adults. You learn to people please. You learn to compare yourself.

When you get honest, you get to choose to live your truth, instead of someone else's.

Remember Your Intention

Years ago, I was wallowing in the self-deprecation that can come before a speaking event. I was about to read a poem I had written in front of six hundred people. I felt insecure because my husband hadn't arrived yet. I made excuses, the way you might when a man stands you up. On top of feeling insecure about his no-show, was the fact that there were six hundred people staring at me from the audience.

Acceptance Moves Inside Out

I felt insecure about the sea of eyes in front of me, and the fact that my husband never ended up watching me speak that day. My intention was to feel accepted. Unfortunately, I had acted out of insecurity that entire day. Turns out, I hadn't told him about the event. Some unconscious part of me lacked the confidence to tell him. He didn't show because he didn't know. Beneath my need to feel accepted by my husband and the audience was a need to accept myself and the message I shared on stage that evening.

I knew that insecure feelings meant I was on shaky ground. I was desperate, so I made myself connect to my intention. I feared rejection because I wanted acceptance. What I truly wanted was for him to be there because I knew him. If he were there, I would know that at least one person in the audience accepted me, no matter how poorly I did.

The positive intention beneath insecurity is acceptance.

The next time you feel insecure, remember and connect to its beautiful intention.

In your current relationship…
What makes you feel insecure?

Whose acceptance do you want?

Why do you need them to accept you?

When you walk through each answer, you realize that you don't need anyone's acceptance in order to accept yourself. If you accept yourself, no one can make you feel insecure. For instance, if you graduated with a 4.0 GPA, you don't feel insecure when someone calls you dumb. You just wonder why they would say that. If you know you are generous, you don't take it personally if an ex calls you selfish. You recognize that he is dealing with his own issues. On the other end of the spectrum, if you know you are terrible at painting or spelling or telling stories, you laugh along when you are teased. Outside opinions and fleeting emotions no longer feel like rejection, but reminders that you haven't yet accepted yourself.

If you feel insecure, take a breath, and remember who you are and what you want. Focus on what you want instead of what others might think of you. Even if you still feel awkward, you don't have to act insecurely. You can act as if your foundation were rooted in something a bit more stable.

Act On Your Intention

The same night I spoke on stage, I felt another layer of insecurity. I wanted the audience to like me. As soon as my insecurity hit a peak, I heard a small voice say within, "Jackie, no one will reject you." Peace washed over me for a moment. Too soon it was cut short by the end of the sentence, "because you haven't let them meet the real you."

I was presenting a fake version of myself to them. I had removed lines from my poem that might rub them the wrong way. I had planned to mimic other poets I had seen succeed. In a desperate attempt to avoid rejection, I made it impossible for them to like me. I had stepped on stage as who I thought they wanted me to be, instead of letting them actually meet me.

How can anyone accept me if I don't show them who I am? In the same way, when you self-edit in your relationship by pretending to be someone you think he will like, you rob him of actually meeting you. You introduce him to a fake version of yourself, which is not the version that the *right guy* will like. The one for you is waiting to meet you. Be brave enough to be yourself.

Take A Tip From A Cupcake

I am addicted to chocolate. If someone doesn't eat chocolate, I assume that they must be allergic. Why else would anyone reject the rich delicacy of cocoa? If you were a cupcake, and some guy didn't like you, you would never apologize for your ingredients. No. You would feel sorry that he couldn't enjoy the tasty sensation you have to offer. You would assume that he had a flaw in *his* design that made him incapable of enjoying you. You, the delectable cupcake that you are, would never lose confidence if he didn't want seconds. You would just assume that some men like chocolate, while others prefer vanilla. If your intention is to be accepted, stop wishing you were vanilla and let him fall in love with you for being chocolate.

Develop Your Skills

Remember when I said all "negative" emotions have a skill-set? Insecurity is no different. Think of the last time you felt insecure. How did your behavior change? How did your thinking change? What skills were you using? You become hyper aware of other's opinions, quick to please, and overly dramatic about other's strengths. While these habits might be showing up in unproductive ways, you can learn to use the same skills in the light.

Here are a few behaviors that insecurity started, but that you can finish:

Worrying about his opinion: Use your ability to notice his opinion as a way to notice negative opinions he has of himself. Encourage him and boost him up with your words.

Withholding parts of yourself that might be rejected: You hold back your opinions, your quirks, and your dance moves when you're feeling awkward. You've probably been withholding since childhood. Although withholding is helpful when you have critical parents or siblings, it is unhelpful now. Use your skill of withholding parts of yourself to withhold the part of you that judges yourself. Same skill set, different outcome.

Comparing yourself to other women: Remember the phrase, "You spot it you got it"? If you spot something you admire in another woman, it means you share that quality with her. Make a list of women who make you feel insecure. Instead of comparing all the ways you don't measure up, compare all the lovely things you share in common.

Spotting your imperfections: I am willing to bet that you have many imperfections that have zero effect on your worth. In these cases, you can unapologetically say, "Yep. I'm sloppy. Yep, I have no sense of direction. Yep, I'm not good at tennis." If you can come clean about some "imperfections" you can practice coming clean about all of them. Find three moments where you can bring your insecurity out of the closet. If you are insecure about being bossy, say unapologetically, "I can be pretty bossy. If I go too far, reel me in." Not only will your partner not care, he will probably laugh along with you.

Once you stop apologizing for yourself, you'll start attracting partners who don't ask you to apologize. You will be able to spot your own imperfections and own them. You will be able to see beautiful people and appreciate them. You will be able to discern his opinion without catering to it. You will finally have a relationship based on secure foundations and authentic communication.

Enjoy Your Saving Grace: Honesty

Inevitably, you will forget everything you just read. When you forget, get honest. Remember Candice's story? Her imagination invented the reason why her date didn't call. An honest perspective is that if he was right for her, he would have called. An honest perspective says that if she loves herself, she can't possibly care about someone who doesn't feel the same way. When I felt insecure on stage, my imagination told me that my husband didn't value my work. An honest perspective reveals that he didn't even know I was speaking. When you are bluntly honest, you will remember that most of your insecurities come from realities you made up.

If you find yourself feeling insecure on your next date, don't fall into conditioned patterns.

Conditioned Response: You put up a wall, stay guarded, and put out an edited version of yourself. After the date, you watch your phone, obsessing over if he liked you. You concoct imaginary hypotheticals about his opinion, and about why he is not texting you.

Upgraded Response: You let him meet you, the real *you*. You don't worry about his opinion of you. You spend the evening getting to know him. If he seems disinterested, you don't take it personally. If he does seem interested, you still don't take it personally. You not only stay open and honest about yourself, but about him. You don't make up hypothetical scenarios about where the night will lead, about what he thinks, or about who else he is dating. You remain honest about what is true versus what is make-believe.

The truth is that your ego loves security. Be on the watch for the following roadblocks between you and an authentic relationship.

Roadblocks On The Route To Honesty

People will guilt-trip you: If you have people pleased men, friends or family for ten years, don't be fooled. They will want that version back. Be honest about who you are *now*.

You will want to people please: You will sense that you didn't please someone enough and your ego will tempt you to self-edit. Don't give into the temptation. These are all forms of manipulation, begging you to be anything except your honest self.

You will mistake his feelings for your feelings: Let me explain. Sometimes you will think you feel insecure around a guy, but really you are picking up on *his* insecurity (see Empathy). Sometimes you are not the awkward one on the date. He just feels awkward. If you feel confident in every situation except with him, you are probably picking up on his feelings, not your own. Be honest about how you feel versus how he feels.

You will feel difficult or needy: Treat your identity like a business. A successful business stays committed to its mission statement. To fulfill your unique mission, you have to be honest about your values. Let your partner love you and all your needs and values. I know you've been trained to not have needs, but the reality is that you do. If you meet a man who makes you feel difficult for having needs, he probably isn't the one. Choose a partner who likes you even when your honesty is not easy. This is not an excuse to be a horror of a girlfriend. This is permission to have needs and to not apologize for them.

Adopt A Lineage Mindset

If you feel especially burdened by insecurity, take your saving grace a step further. Don't be honest for you, be honest as an act of service for the women who will come after you. When your daughter asks you how you and daddy fell in love, do you want to tell her that you became everything he wanted you to be, changing your views on life, your ambitions, and your cup size to gain his nearly unattainable validation? I hope not. Tell that little girl you gave one thousand zero ducks about his opinion, and he fell head over heels in love with the *real* you.

PART FOUR
Dating

*"Reckless words pierce like a sword,
but the tongue of the wise brings healing."*
– Proverbs

9

Anger: Why Can't I Control My Temper?

♥ ♥ ♥

Anger is never a good justification to disempower, hurt or belittle.
Anger is fuel to fight for your deepest needs.

I broke up with him, but now I'm the one crying. It's been a year, but I still haven't fully grieved. I wanted him to see someone knew, but now I want to kill the girl in his photos. I thought I'd feel happy, but now I'm pissed that he's the one smiling.

Kaylee and her boyfriend had walked that sharp edge between breaking up and getting married. They seesawed for five years, but every time she brought up marriage, he said he wasn't the marrying kind. "Why fix what isn't broken?" Well, she wanted kids, and she wanted them to have a committed dad. She left him. A few months after their break-up, she saw a picture of her ex with his new fiancé. His anti-marriage campaign had apparently ended when he met a different kind of woman.

It hurt. When I picked up the phone, her voice barely made its way over to me. She thought it shouldn't upset her. She broke up with him, right? I asked what I always ask when someone is having a hard time grieving. "Are you angry?"

"Angry? No. I don't really get angry." She seemed insulted by my suggestion. I let it go, but as we worked through her grief we inevitably hit the third stage: anger. Until Kaylee worked through all five stages of her sadness, her grief would feel stunted, incomplete.

If you are in a relationship and feel stuck in disappointment or grief, you might have unprocessed anger. If you find yourself in a never-ending cycle of "pissed off," you might be dealing with unprocessed grief. If you feel stuck in a cycle of self-sabotage, you might want to look into this sticky stage of rage.

Kaylee had a lot to be angry about in her situation. Since she felt more comfortable suppressing her anger, she was left feeling disempowered and upset. When Kaylee and I worked through the positive side of owning her anger, she transformed. I barely recognized her when she called me a few months later. Instead of sounding timid, she seemed self-assured. She stopped being passive aggressive and let go of her unconscious grudges. Instead, she felt her anger and used it to fight for her needs. The Kaylee who called me back had mastered the art of using her anger in the light.

Anger has been misused to the point that you probably opt to suppress it. Maybe you've been personally hurt by someone's anger. Maybe you've been judged for being angry. Maybe you've spent years trying to fix your passive aggressive tendencies. I get it. While it might sound unrealistic, you might not need to fix anything.

ANGER IN THE DARK	ANGER IN THE LIGHT
Disempowers	Empowers those who cannot speak up for themselves
Assumes everyone is out to get you	Assumes others simply aren't able to meet your needs
Violates others' rights	Advocates for needs and rights of self and others
Becomes explosive and destructive when boundaries are crossed	Sets boundaries
Immaturely points out partner's flaws	Rationally and productively points out partner's areas of growth
Becomes passive aggressive and guilt-tripping to get needs met	Becomes open and vulnerable about needs
Desires to prove partner wrong	Desires to work with partner to bring about what is right
Intends to harm and belittle	Intends to reclaim needs that have been lost

If you are currently dating, and you are noticing your anger patterns rearing their ugly head, I have a challenge. Think about your pattern as an opportunity to upgrade. The anger is coming up for a reason. Do you want to stifle the anger? Do you want to judge yourself for feeling it? Or, do you want to listen to what your feelings are trying to tell you? Anger means you have an inner advocate that wants to fight for you. If you ignore her, she will disempower you and your partner. She will keep you locked in cycles of loss, blame, and (not so obvious) self-punishment.

Anger's cycle of self-sabotage will end when you introduce her to her partner in crime, empowerment. It might seem far-fetched, but by the end of the chapter, you will embrace anger as fuel to fight for what you've always wanted. Your anger will help you advocate for your deepest needs and your partner's needs. She will help you set boundaries. She will help you process your feelings of grief and bitterness. She will demand that you feel seen and heard in your relationship. Let's begin by seeing and hearing what Ms. Anger has to say.

Unplug Judgment

Rachel was a clinician when she came to me to work on her relationship status, single and over it. She had one goal, "I'm ready to meet my husband."

She blamed her weight and addictive personality. As we looked into her "readiness for a husband," a very strong feeling erupted. She was angry. Why was she still single? Why did her not-so-put-together friends have partners? Why couldn't she kick her habits? Why was she still dealing with the same issues? Why!? If Rachel wanted to move through this season, she was going to have to feel her anger. The problem was that she judged herself for having such an ugly feeling. Ugly or not, the first step was to give herself some grace. As you read about the possible reasons Rachel judged herself so hard, filter the stereotypes through your own experience.

Anger's Stereotypes

Like most women, Rachel learned to judge her anger because of culturally ingrained beliefs about it. Here are a few of my favorite (inaccurate) stereotypes about anger:

Anger is unattractive and ugly
Anger is not "lady-like"

Anger hurts people

Anger brings out the worst in people

Anger makes me do and say things I regret

Anger makes me sound like my mother

Anger makes me nag

Of course Rachel judged her anger. No one wants to be ugly, unforgiving and nagging. She had seen people lash out. It wasn't pretty, but bare with me when I say: anger itself is not ugly. Yelling at a child out of anger is ugly. Hitting a partner out of anger is ugly. Catch the difference? How people *act* when they misuse anger is ugly, not anger itself. Just because most people are damaging and condescending when angry, doesn't mean you have to be. You can learn to express anger in a calm and productive way.

Anger Doesn't Have To Hurt

Anger can't hurt you. People can hurt you. People you know have done horrific things because of their ill relationship with anger. In my experience, angry people are not scary. Angry people are scared. They are so scared that they have to disempower you to feel an ounce of power themselves.

Rachel judged anger because of the way she saw "role models" act on it. She is not alone. Answer the following questions in order to uncover unconscious judgments you have toward anger: Has a partner hurt you while angry? How do you feel about them? Have you ever been angry with a partner? How did you feel about yourself afterward? Are you proud of how you look and act when angry? What would people say about you if they saw you at your angriest?

You just wrote down all your judgments about anger. You'll want to surrender each before you can fully feel it, release it, and bring it into the light.

When Rachel was a kid, she witnessed some horrific displays of anger. If she broke a rule, she had 20 seconds to prep before her mom verbally sliced her down. Because Rachel had sworn to never be like her mom, she judged herself. She would cut her partner down with her words in a frighteningly familiar tone and spend the next hour swallowing her rage.

I swallowed my anger for a long time. This stifled my growth, and my ability to sustain an easy and calm relationship. I had to face my anger patterns if I wanted to leave them in the past. If you want to leave anger in the past, learn to separate this emotion from the actions it inspires.

SEPARATE ANGER AND ACTIONS EXERCISE

1. When was the last time you were angry with your partner? Give the moment a title.
2. Describe or draw the anger as vividly as possible:
3. How did you act when you felt angry? Make a list of the subtle and not-so-subtle actions you took:
4. When you took each action, what did you want?
5. Now, cross out actions that don't get you what you want. Write what you can do in the future.

Don't blame anger for bad behavior, and don't blame yourself for being angry. Commit to giving yourself grace, while taking conscious control of your choices. Once you trust yourself to run the show, you won't feel threatened listening to what anger has to say.

Plug Into Anger's Message: What Have I Lost?

Out of all the emotions, clients have the easiest time describing their anger. I've heard women describe their anger as a fire or heat in their stomach. Anger feels fiery because she's fuel, a fuel to fight for what you want. If you look into the etymology of the word 'want,' you'll find that want is a synonym of *lack*. If you *want* something, you *lack* it. You get angry because you want to get what you lack back.

If you struggle with anger, notice when and where you feel her. Do you feel angry when your partner ignores you? Is it because you want (aka lack) feeling seen in that moment? Do you feel angry that you are still single? Is it because you want (aka lack) the love you deserve? Are you angry when he lies to you? Is it because you want (aka lack) the trust you deserve? Anger arises when you lack what know you deserve.

The positive message behind anger is that you want and deserve something. Anger reminds you to fight for what you deserve.

If you know you lack what you deserve, you will get angry enough to fight for it. In my experience, anger grows in direct relationship to lack. Susie might want her partner to do the dishes. Mary might want her partner to do the dishes. Susie stays calm while Mary flips out because Mary feels like he *never* does the dishes. Her lack is greater, so her anger is greater.

The reason she is so upset about this seemingly minor situation is that a deeper need is not being met. She couldn't care less about dishes. She actually cares about feeling appreciated. As Malcolm X once said, "When people are sad, they don't do anything. They just cry over their condition. But when they get angry, they bring about a change." It is your anger, that rises up and reminds you to fight for what you deserve from the person who took it. Whether the situation feels major or minor, you must get clear on who is to blame for your feelings of lack. Blaming your partner is rarely accurate.

Real And Historical Lack

Remember Kaylee's story? She was upset because her boyfriend didn't want to marry her. She didn't feel chosen. Was her partner stealing her feelings of "chosen", or was someone else to blame? We explored the answer in my office. Kaylee was a middle child. She always felt pegged up against her siblings. She felt that no matter how perfect she was, she was never chosen by her parents. When her partner entered the scene, he was up against 10 years of accumulated lack. He was a trigger to the void that began in childhood. While this might sound like a problem, we actually used the issue as an opportunity to release years of pent up rage.

Read the list of common areas of lack that trigger anger. As you read the list, circle the losses that resonate with you. If memories crop up from the past, make note. Commit to taking the time to mindfully process any feelings of grief and anger. Instead of waiting for your partner to trigger your feelings, use this time to safely process the lack you dealt with as a kid. I am here as a resource if you need to process with someone.

Common Losses That Trigger Anger

Respect

Expectations

Acceptance

Control

Love

Safety

Trust

Promises

Being a priority

_____

Related memories:

Anger is a GPS system steering you toward what you need and deserve. GPS systems aren't created to drive. Drivers are created to listen and steer accordingly. When anger boils, you have two options. One, you can blame your partner for the lack you feel, disempowering him while disabling yourself from getting what you want. Two, you can receive the message about what you want, express your need, and seek a conscious way to fill it.

Instead of fighting *against* the lack, fight *for* what you need.

Ask yourself:

Why am I angry?
What have I lost?
What do I lack?
What do I need? Deserve? Expect from this relationship?
What is the best way to fill this need?

The purpose of anger is to say "Hey, you've lost something here that you want and deserve. Go get it back." Yelling, blaming and fighting rarely will get back what you lost. To reclaim what you lost, you have to get honest with yourself and your partner.

Get Honest

When my college boyfriend cheated on me I wanted him to "pay" for what he did. I wanted him to pay with guilt and repercussions. When you get honest about your anger, you realize that you are less angry about your partner did and angrier that he is getting away with it. Just think of a time when your partner upset you, but felt badly and apologized. Then, think of a moment when he upset you and felt absolutely no remorse. When did you feel angrier? In my experience, anger grows when your partner doesn't pay.

The predicament is that your partner may never apologize. He may never feel remorse. He may never face any tangible repercussion for hurting you. If you wait for him to "pay," you will hold on to anger the rest of your life. You will end up paying for what he wasn't brave enough to face.

THE PRICE YOU PAY EXERCISE

Take a moment to recall an event that deeply enraged you, a moment where you felt completely justified in your anger. If recognizing anger is not one of your strengths, use these trigger words to target a moment.

Trigger Words

I can't believe he…

How dare he…

He deserves the worst for…

I am so justified…

1. Once you recall an enraging event, give it a title _____
2. On a scale of 0-10, how angry does this event make you? ___
3. Then, get honest:
   - What did he do that was wrong?
   - Do you want to see him "pay"?
   - In what quiet and loud ways did you punish him? Silent treatment? Cold shoulder? Nitpick? Give more attention to others?
   - Why? What did you want?
   - Did this punishment get you what you want?

With this event in mind, tap through the calming EFT pressure points located in the back of the book. Keep tapping, and be blatantly honest about your feelings. By tapping and talking, you release hardwired habits that lock you in cycles of self-sabotage. The following sentence starters will help you get really honest as you tap.

I'm justified

He is in the wrong, because…

Because of him, I lost… (trust, confidence, safety)

Because of him, I'll never get back my...
And when I get angry I punish him by...
I withhold love by...
I withhold kindness by...
I have to stay angry about this because...

How do you feel when you talk and "tap" through the prompts? How does it feel to say you are "justified"? Justification gives you permission to disempower and misuse anger. Demanding your partner "pay" will never get you what you need. Owning how you feel and letting it go will set you up to think of more productive solutions. Tapping while voicing your justification in this safe way won't reinforce your anger, but releases the steam. Hopefully, you feel your anger dissipating, and see calm and conscious ways to ask for what you want.

Take a tip from an activist. Don't wait for your past or present partners to "pay" before you claim what you want. If MLK waited for the white supremacists to apologize or pay, he would still be waiting. When you get honest, you bring cycles of punishment to the surface where you can let them go and move ahead toward intentions that actually fulfill your needs.

Remember Your Intention

When you are angry, you are being signaled that you have lost something. Your intention is to go get what you have lost back from a source much higher than the small person who stole it from you.

The intention behind anger is to reclaim what you have lost.

One of my clients, Emily, was 24 years old when a therapy session revealed to her a memory that had been locked in a trauma capsule for two decades. When she was four, her stepfather had sexually abused her. In the first session, we explored the shock and grief of being a victim of unsolicited violence. In the next session, anger roared. Of course she was angry. She had not only lost her sense of safety and justice, but her image of a father. Everything she thought was real became fuzzy. She had two choices: Verbally *attack* her parents for not making her feel safe, or *fight for* her right to feel safe, which would empower her and other women in similar situations.

FIGHT FOR IT EXERCISE

The next time you feel angry, ask yourself:

1. What have I lost?
2. Why does this make me angry? What am I against in this situation? What values, traits, behaviors, ways of communicating or relating am I against?
3. Then flip the script. If I am *against* this, what must I be *for* in this situation?
4. What am I willing to fight for? What values, traits, behaviors, and ways of communicating or relating?

Emily was against violation, injustice, and being robbed of her innocence. She was against feeling unsafe because of choices she never made. She was for justice, and for honesty. She was for transparency and owning up to actions. She was for respecting others, even when they don't have the ability to ask for respect.

Fear reminds you what you are up *against*. Intention reminds you what you are willing to stand *for*. Fight *for* what you want instead of fighting *against* what you don't want. The simple change in language is a legacy shaking change in your relationship.

Act On Your Intention

While Emily wanted to leave a legacy of justice and feminine safety, she was heading toward it in a painful way. Up until our work together, Emily had unconsciously carried twenty extra pounds as a way to protect herself from male attention. Carrying the weight and resentment was clearly not helping. When she got clear about her intentions, she was able to make empowered changes. She used her anger as fuel to empower other women with similar experiences. She used her story to write a script that shed light on the prevalence of sexual abuse. She poked fun at the absurd ways women are taught to feel guilty for men's choices. The more she performed her show, the less resentment she felt toward disrespectful men. The more she vocalized her female audience members' right for innocence, the less she harbored shame when men guilted her. Acting on her truth, instead of reacting with anger, changed her relationship with men, her past, her body and her own purpose.

Own Your Deserving

The best way to fight for what you want is to know you are worthy of it. If your partner withholds respect, but you know you deserve respect, you will fight for it. If he withholds love, but you know you deserve love, you will ask for love, and leave if he can't give it to you. You don't have to fight against the withholder, but you can fight for the object of your desire. The only reason you would fight against him would be to prove you deserved what is already rightfully yours. That being said, if you are stuck in an anger cycle, you can pull yourself out by reconnecting to what you deserve, knowing you are worthy, and then acting.

Ask yourself:

What need do I want to be met?
Am I worthy of it? Yes!
What is my intended outcome?
What is the fastest route to that outcome?

Source of Anger	Against/ For	Intention	Act on Anger	Act on Intention
I'm sick of being single	I am against loneliness/ I am for a good relationship	I intend to be in a good relationship	I act desperate	I will create a good relationship with myself and the people currently in my life
My ex cheated on me	I am against deception/ I am f or transparency and respect	I intend to be with a loyal and respectful partner	I left nasty comments on the girl's social media and I refuse to trust all men	I choose men who are honest and respectful, with no history of cheating. I advocate for respecting women

Source of Anger	Against/ For	Intention	Act on Anger	Act on Intention
My partner never remembers our anniversary	I am against a lack of awareness/ I am for honoring each other	I intend to celebrate our love every year	I guilt trip and hold this over his head for months	I send a flirty note to his office a week before our anniversary as a reminder
My partner spends too much money	I am against irresponsibility and debt/ I am for discipline	I intend to be responsible with money and have savings for travel	I nag him about how many times he has eaten out this week	I get him excited about a trip and set up a plan to save each month
I was abused in the past	I am against abuse/ I am for safety and respect	I intend to be respected by men… and women!	I distrust all men and lash out when my partner doesn't respect that	I volunteer for a non-profit that advocates for women's health and safety

Acting on anger might feel good momentarily, but it rarely brings you what you want. Commit to regularly acting on what you want, instead of fighting against what you don't want. As you read the following examples, jot down your own ideas.

Like Emily, make your intentions a part of your lifestyle. Better yet, take action that empowers other women, women who might not have your fire.

Develop Your Skills

In the light, anger is the emotion of activists. While you might not be an NGO founder, you are an activist in your own relationship. Anger fights for your rights and rises up when you don't get them. If she causes you to disempower your partner, stop and breathe. Get creative and find a way to stand up for yourself in a way that gets you what you want without stooping. A good rule of thumb is to make sure anger is leading to empowerment, not disempowerment.

In the dark anger: disempowers, belittles, punishes, blames, condescends, and harbors resentment.

In the light anger: empowers, holds accountable, frees, sets boundaries, and lets go.

Emily may have wanted to find her violator, and teepee his house, but is that going to empower her to experience lasting justice? Is that going to empower other women? No. Instead, she used her voice to empower other women to speak up about their past. She set boundaries with herself about how she would relate to her memories. She held men accountable with the script she wrote, but freed trustworthy men to rewrite her biases.

If you still can't imagine how anger can be beneficial, Google the 'About' page of your favorite non-profit. Most social justice campaigns come out of an individual's anger toward loss. The A21 campaign, a human trafficking non-profit, has freed thousands of women from the sex trade. Guess who started that non-profit? Christine Caine, a woman born into injustice.

Create lists of people in relationships who have used anger to empower themselves and others. Christine Caine is one woman. Emily is a second. Add yourself to the list and write how you can use your anger to reclaim what you have lost. This list will come in handy when fear arises to pull you back from your conditioned way of reacting.

Enjoy Your Saving Grace: Empowerment

Inevitably, you will feel anger about your partner in not-so-critical moments. He will forget your birthday, or care more about his career than you, or hurt you in some way. Before you act on conditioned ways of relating to anger, enjoy your saving grace: Empowerment.

Ask, how can I use this anger to empower my partner and myself?

Did he forget to ask about the big career switch at dinner? Did you feel disrespected? Feel the anger and empower yourself to speak up and share how important it is for him to care about your work. You won't be passive aggressive or nit-picky if you unapologetically voice your needs.

Imagine that your partner notices that you are angry and pent up. He asks you, "What is wrong?"

Conditioned Response: You say, "Nothing. I just thought you'd care enough to ask about my day. I should have known. You're too into your stuff to remember."

Upgraded Response: You say, "I need to feel like you support my goals the way I try to support yours. I'm really proud of what happened at work today and I want to share it with you."

The first response is passive and belittling. The second response empowers the partner to meet your needs. Make a commitment to how you want to use your anger. Write what needs you will ask *for* in your relationship and *for* other women. Feeling anger and staying empowered is easier said than done. Prep yourself by understanding the following roadblocks.

Roadblocks On The Route To Empowerment

He will intentionally disempower you: When a man seems to go out of his way to put you down, disrespect you, hurt you, or lie to you, empower yourself. Empower yourself by not playing victim to his choices. Assume that his actions or lack of actions don't reflect you.

You will want revenge: Getting revenge is stooping to his level. Empower yourself to stay on higher ground. The truth is, revenge won't get your needs met.

You will judge yourself for having needs: I've repeated this statement multiple times. When you feel needy, speak up for your needs, not out of selfishness, but out of generosity. When your needs are met, you have more to give back to your partner. The following needs are universal, so stop judging yourself when you want them to be met.

Common Unmet Needs That Create Anger:

The need for respect

The need for peace

The need for safety

The need for value

The need for provision

The need for justice and fairness

The need for certainty

The need to feel seen, heard and understood

The need to feel loved and valued

Owning what you need empowers you to give. Asking your partner to meet your needs empowers him to feel valuable. Men love feeling needed. Empower him by asking.

He will do that thing he always says he will stop doing: If the little things make you most angry, empower yourself by being passive. Passive is different than passive aggressive. Passive means to not actively respond or resist. When he leaves the toilet seat up, feel your anger without acting on your anger. Your anger most likely has nothing to do with him and more to do with a loss he is triggering from your past. In these small situations, you will find more power in letting it go because these are examples of historical lack.

He will make a mistake: If you are in the habit of blaming your partner when he makes a mistake, breathe. Anger does not have to be about punishment. Think good coach bad coach. Which coaching style motivates you more? Encouragement or ridicule? Empower him by replacing punishment with encouragement.

Let Anger Call Up Real Men

My love, your anger is powerful. Use it to voice your deepest needs. Declaring your needs empowers real men to rise up and meet the challenge, and empowers other women who are looking to you as an example. If your anger is more subtle, and comes out as irritation and small judgments, the next chapter is for you.

10

Judgment: I Can't Stand When He...

Judgment is not the ability to see what you like and don't like about your partner. Judgment is a mirror, and a moment to recognize what you have rejected in yourself.

He didn't apologize for who he was. He didn't apologize for what he wanted, or where he was going, or why he deserved to go. I fell in love with him for it, him being my husband. After he proposed though, judgment swept in. Loud and aggressive, I nitpicked him for being arrogant. I rolled my eyes at his stories. I stubbornly pushed my agenda on him as if he wasn't a grown man with a full life he led before me. I complained about his lack of cleaning skills. I worried about his budget. I thought he needed to mature, become more self-aware, change.

In between proposal and wedding day I learned a crucial lesson. The traits I judge and suppress in my husband are the traits I have suppressed in myself.

Humans attract partners who embody their suppressed traits. For example, women who are perfectionists inevitably attract men who seem immature and un-invested in their growth. Insecure women attract narcissistic men. Type A women attract carefree men. Is this a punishment? No. You are sent to people who will inevitably lead you to be more whole.

Of course the traits that attract you to your partner are the very thing that will threaten to push you away. Confidence becomes arrogance. Carefree becomes a lack of self-awareness. Talkative becomes a lack of care for someone else. Sweet becomes soft. Self-aware becomes insecure. Doting becomes controlling. Why do you attract men you will inevitably judge? Because your true self wants to grow and learn from your opposite.

JUDGMENT IN THE DARK	JUDGMENT IN THE LIGHT
Gossips	Uses words to lift partner up
Nitpicks	Forgives
Impatient and self righteous	Patient and curious
Tries to be right	Reveals opportunity to try to be more loving
Demeans partner for differences and "weaknesses"	Appreciates partner's' differences
Tries to prove your ways as right, smarter, or better	You try to get curious and learn from others
Condescends self and partner for imperfections	Sees imperfections as an opportunity to practice unconditional love

Warning: This chapter is difficult for most to swallow. Skip it if you don't think you can hack it, or pause and swallow a humility pill.

If you drop this book remembering one thing, remember that what you judge in your partner, you have already judged in yourself. When you feel judgment, irritation or stubbornness rise up in you, get ready to find an untapped gift you've never let yourself enjoy.

When you don't understand judgment, you will find yourself repelled from your partner for the same qualities that first made him attractive. When you learn to respond to judgmental feelings in an upgraded way, you will create more ease and play in your relationship. By the end of this chapter, you will pair your judgmental muscle with its toned wing woman, curiosity.

Before you begin, take note: What qualities do you find most unattractive in your partner? What traits are you justified in judging? On a scale of 0-10, how strong is your judgment about each trait?

By the end of the chapter, you will see these traits from a completely different perspective. Dare I say, when you do the inner work, your partner will change even more than you change.

Unplug Judgment

You hate being judged. Why would you want to condone it in yourself? Pause. The judgment you hate is the kind of judgment that is used in the dark, the judgment that belittles, that condescends, that criticizes. Before I tell you the opportunity waiting in judgment, I want to help you remove the stigma that she is all bad. Before you badmouth this feeling entirely, educate yourself on her role in evolution.

The Evolution Of Judgment

Toxic bad-mouthing is not only hardwired into our culture, but wired into your evolution. Experts say that judgment and gossip were used in tribal societies as a way to move up the social hierarchy. If you can spot flaws in another, you have evidence that you are better than them. Being "better" secures your rank on the relationship ladder. Today, judging your mate might not guarantee your social status, but it gives you a quick ego-boost.

The second reason gossip is evolutionarily beneficial is that gossip bonds people together. Gossip acts as a bonding rope that ties the conversationalists together with a rope of judgment. Think of the last time you tittered over a glass of wine with the girls. You felt closer to them, but at the expense of your partner. You have been culturally and biologically wired to judge your partner. While it made sense in the past, judgment is no longer beneficial.

UNCONSCIOUS PERKS OF JUDGMENT EXERCISE
A) **Ego Boost:**
   1. When do you judge your partner?
   2. In what ways do you get to feel good about yourself, your choices, or your way of doing things by judging him?

      As you notice your source of judgment, notice what ego boost you get to feel. Do you judge his style? That must mean your style is better. Do you judge him when he mispronounces words? You must be an excellent wordsmith. If you are judging him for an ego boost, find a healthier way to compliment yourself besides throwing him under the bus.

B) **Gossip:**
   1. When was the last time you gossiped about your partner with a friend?
   2. How did the gossip impact your relationship?
   3. Was badmouthing him harmless? Or did gossip create toxicity in your relationship?

4. If "harmless" gossip is sabotaging your love, why are you still doing it?

When you recognize that your words have power, you become more intentional about how you use them.

Plug Into Judgment's Message: What Is Bad? What Is Good?

Sorry to say, if you judge his mannerisms, habits or quirks as bad, you are bound to judge them in yourself.

The positive message behind judgment: Self-awareness, acceptance, and growth.

For a moment, pause and pretend you could only follow one rule: love yourself and other people. If you felt judgment rise up toward your partner, you wouldn't say, "Oh my. That is so horrible when he xyz." You would think, "Looks like I haven't learned to love that part of him yet, or that part of myself yet." Do you want to use feelings of judgment to condemn your partner? Or as an opportunity to love him and yourself more? The stronger the judgment, the greater the challenge to reflect, accept and grow.

Challenge accepted.

Judgment Heals

According to relationship expert Harville Hendrix, 90% of relationship frustrations have to do with past wounding. Your partner may not intentionally wound you, but he unknowingly scrapes off your scabs. His shortcomings remind you to address old wounds that want to heal. They coined the concept as the Imago, a theory that continues to save my own relationship.

Harville Hendrix and Helen LaKelly describe the Imago in their book *Making Marriage Simple*: "Romantic love delivers us into the passionate arms of someone who will ultimately trigger the same frustrations we had with our parents, for the best possible reason! Doing so brings our childhood wounds to the surface so they can be healed." If your partner constantly triggers your buttons, you are in luck. You are being prompted to look within and heal old wounds before they manifest as more difficult relationships.

Harper came to me frustrated. She was fed up with her boyfriend's lack of self-awareness. She liked that he was driven, but it seemed like he cared more about his career than her. She always left dates feeling unseen and unvalued. I mean, she had big career goals too, and she wasn't going to let anyone belittle them. When Harper explored her Imago, she found that he was not the first to make her feel invalidated and disregarded. She grew up with a mother who could not see past her own nose. Her mom did her best, but she was too absorbed in her dating drama and stack of bills to be there for her three girls. Harper grew up feeling like an after-thought. Her partner's disinterest in her career plans, and her judgment of his disinterest was an opportunity to explore and heal from a childhood that left her feeling like a second priority. Both her mom and her partner seemed to put themselves first, but when she explored her past with me, she saw that her mom and her partner were just doing their best.

When I first started working with Harper's Imago, she felt like she was being punished for unmet childhood wounds. The Imago, which causes you to date men you wind up judging, is not a punishment. The Imago is an opportunity to face your demons. When you free your demons, you will either heal enough to leave your partner, or heal to the point in which his habits no longer bother you.

THE IMAGO EXERCISE

Part one: For the following questions, imagine you are nine years old or younger.

> 1a. How does your caregiver treat you? Where do they excel? Where do they fall short?
>
> 1b. What about their personality, behaviors or habits makes you most frustrated?
>
> 1c. How does your father make you feel?
>
> 1d. How does your mother make you feel?

Part two: For the following questions, imagine your typical love relationship:

> 2a. How does your partner treat you? Where do they excel? Where do they fall short?
>
> 2b. What about their personality, behaviors or habits makes you most frustrated?
>
> 2c. How does your partner make you feel?

Read over your answers. Notice similarities between your partner and your parental figures. Although you might not be "dating your father," you are probably dating the unmet needs your father and mother never filled.

Normally, your partner's negative traits don't hurt you, but they reflect a trait that did hurt you as a kid. Imagine that you are a kid again. Ask your childhood self why those traits are so frustrating. Erica's mom neglected her in the pursuit of a career. When she saw this trait reflected in her partner, her red flags waved. Realistically, his investment in his career was not neglectful of her. She just perceived it that way. His seeming lack of care for her goals was just her perception. When she addressed her childhood needs with me, she saw his career drive as enthusiasm, instead of neglect.

The majority of people are unwilling to face their demons because they'd rather demonize their partner. Knowing you, you rarely choose the normal route. Let's set you up to beat the 50% and upgrade this emotion.

Get Honest

Imagine that you are five and you proudly get in front of the classroom to show off a song you wrote. The kids laugh. They whisper about you. In that moment, with your kid-like perspective, you wish you hadn't been so sure of yourself. You wish you hadn't been so confident because now you feel humiliated. You group confidence, arrogance, and humiliation together in one "bad" category. Then, you vow to never use these "bad" traits in the future.

As you get older you say you want to feel confident with men. For some reason, you struggle to feel confident because something about it feels arrogant. You are unaware of the unconscious story that has been playing in your head about arrogance and humiliation. You look at your partner who is shamelessly confident and write him off as egotistical. If he is loud and unapologetic, you judge him for his pride. It never occurs to you that you are no longer seeing him clearly but through the lens of your own suppressed confidence.

If you judge his narcissism, selfishness, greed or laziness, you most likely met each trait long before you met him. These traits hurt you as a kid, and your ego will do everything it can to protect you from further damage. What do you judge in your partner? Do these traits seem familiar? Have you suppressed them in yourself? Take time to explore your answers.

The Shadow Self

In Debbie Ford's book, *The Dark Side of the Light Chasers*, she describes the shadow, a Jungian Psychological concept. She says,

> All of your so-called faults, all the things which you don't like about yourself are your greatest assets. They are simply over amplified. The volume has been turned up a bit too much, that's all. Just turn down the volume a little. Soon, you—and everyone else—will see your weaknesses as your strengths, your 'negatives' as your 'positives.' They will become wonderful tools, ready to work for you rather than against you. All you have to do is learn to call on these personality traits in amounts that are appropriate to the moment.

For a moment, imagine that you had to make a list of personal goals. You might include 1) confidence 2) good boundaries 3) speak up for myself. Great goals. Then, imagine you had to make a list of personal traits you don't like in your partner. You might write 1) his ego 2) selfish tendencies 3) Too talkative. Do you spot the irony? While you want confidence, you judge his over-confidence. Your partner is role modeling the very traits you want.

I know it's hard to not judge him for traits you never let yourself enjoy, but here is your chance. Enjoy them! Enjoy him! Figure out how his "negative" traits can have a positive impact in your life. Then, practice using the skills he has in a way that works for you. For example, he might be pretty cocky, but can you learn from his confidence? He might talk a bit too much, but can you learn to mimic his unapologetic enthusiasm? The more you embrace the good and bad of every personality trait, the more whole you will become.

Lets' practice working with your shadow with a trait that the majority of my readers judge: narcissism. First, make a list of characteristics that describe an egomaniac. Be objective. What skills have egomaniacs mastered?

They think their opinion matters
They believe they should have influence
They believe in themselves, their gifts, and their mission
They embrace praise and acceptance but don't need it
They don't take no for an answer
They have a powerful presence
They are focused on their priorities
They charge forward without getting distracted by others hesitation
They steamroll opposition
They don't bat an eye at criticism

Great. Now write one way you can use each quality to benefit your relationship.

Look at that! Getting honest with yourself about what you don't like about your partner doesn't make you a bad person. Getting honest helps you see the beneficial side of his skills. With this objective attitude, you stop judging him so much. In turn, you stop judging yourself so much. The habits that used to push your buttons will no longer bother you.

You know the phrase, "You can't knock it until you've tried it?" Well, the same is true for personality traits. Before you judge a man, walk in his shoes. Is he immature? Let yourself be not-so-responsible for an hour. Is he scattered? Let yourself go a day without a strict plan. The more you let yourself walk in his shoes, the more compassionate you will be toward him, and his flaws. I'm not saying you have to change your personality completely. I'm just saying that every person has something to offer you, and every trait has something to teach you. Get curious about the beneficial skills within his most annoying traits, and before you know it, your man's unapologetic behaviors won't bother you so much. Nitpick less. Love more.

Remember Your Intention

Don't be so messy. Be more organized. Don't spend so much money. Be more mature. Don't be so careless. Be more responsible. Every time you judge your partner, you have a clear idea about why he is wrong, and why you are right. **The intention of judgment is to point out what is right,** but "right" is relative. He is probably in the wrong sometimes, but is judging him for it right?

Nitpicking rarely ends well. Instead of criticizing him for what he *isn't* doing, encourage him toward what he can do better. That being said, you are not his mother, or teacher, or therapist. Use your judgmental eye responsibly. Focus on what you think is right, and instead of critiquing his shortcomings, applaud his growth.

Complete the following sentences:
I can't stand when he…
I judge him most when he…
I am most embarrassed when he…
I would be embarrassed if he pointed out my…
I hope no one ever describes me as…

Now that you have each written, take a moment to notice the traits you value based on your judgment. Can you not stand the way he dresses? Good to know. You intend to be stylish. Do you judge his lack of generosity? Okay. You intend to be generous. Are you embarrassed by his long stories? Maybe you intend to be more humble. The next time you judge your partner, focus on your underlying intentions. Intentions point out your values, and knowing your values will help you value your partner.

There are many routes to your ideal destination. Encouragement and positivity are the far more productive road. When your partner feels you judging him behind his back, he will be far less open to hearing you out. By focusing on long-term values instead of short-term pet peeves, your relationship will embody far more of your "rights" than your "wrongs". There will be less frustration. There will be less, "I don't even know where this fight started." There will be less of a reason to fight because you are focused on all the ways he is embodying what you want.

Act On Your Intention

Where attention goes, energy flows, so I challenge you to focus on what you do want before saying another judgmental word about what you don't want. In the last step, you identified your values. Now the challenge is to act on them.

Partners Are Supposed To Push Your Buttons

"He is just so irresponsible with what he makes! An artist who can barely afford rent shouldn't be eating out every day! I'm sick of being his financial planner." Up until this point, all Allison could do was react with judgment, nagging him about his splurges and passive-aggressively commenting on his pricey night out with the boys. As you might guess, nagging wasn't motivating him to change.

Most often working through your judgments brings you closer to your partner. As you explore your shadow and your Imago, you heal. Wounds from childhood heal. He no longer has to push your buttons, because the buttons no longer work. He doesn't even have to change, because what frustrates you has changed.

Disclaimer: Some Imago and shadow work break up a bad relationship, but minor frustrations are usually a sign of internal issues.

Allison called my office that day because her partner's spending "issues" were making her question if she had made some kind of mistake.

Should it be this frustrating? Does it have to be this hard? Is it ridiculous to want him to be perfect? Nitpicking hadn't been effective, so she was open to exploring alternate roads. We worked through these questions in her first few sessions. As you read Allison's answers, replace italics with your own words.

> Me: What frustrates you?
> Allison: *His spending*
> Me: How do you feel when he *spends so much?*
> Allison: *Like I don't have control. I feel helpless.*
> Me: How do you want to feel?
> Allison: *I want to feel safe.*
> Me: Can you feel *safe* now, even if he keeps *spending?*
> Allison: *No! Even if I do everything right, it doesn't matter because he could just spend it all. No matter how good I am, the ball will inevitably drop.*
> Me: Is this the first time you've felt like *the ball could drop, even if you do everything right?*

The short answer was no. Let's just say Allison's dad wasn't the best with handling cash. Financial instability had laced its way through her parent's relationship. In fact, Allison later revealed that her mom divorced her dad over money issues. Of course she was having a hard time with her boyfriend. His spending habits were triggering an old wound that began when she saw mom do everything right, and still, the ball dropped. Her mom had been responsible and strategic with money, and what did she get in return? Debt and divorce papers.

Setting childhood aside, Allison needed to release past fears so she could speak to her partner from a present and productive place. When we worked through her money fears, she stopped nagging him, and he asked her advice on money matters. She stopped questioning him, and he stopped defending his spending. He started using a budget. He wanted to eat at home more with her. In the weeks to follow, she couldn't tell if he changed or she changed, but something huge shifted.

Was he responding to her less loaded requests? Was she more open to seeing all that he did right? Did her internal healing literally heal his spending issues? I'm not sure. I do know that by honoring her deep need for financial stability and safety, she was forced to deal with the fears that made safety feel impossible. Clearing her fears of instability made it easier for Allison to stop nitpicking the spending she hated, and start asking for the stability she always wanted. Her inner work allowed her to ask from an empowered place, instead of a combative place. Her partner responded well to the difference.

If Allison hadn't worked through her frustrations, she not only would have missed out on a beautiful relationship but on a sense of safety and freedom she didn't know was possible.

How Can You Act On Your Intention?

Step one: Enjoy your values. Enjoy your humility, generosity or compassion. Just because your partner doesn't naturally value the same things, doesn't mean he should stop you from enjoying them.

Step two: Make the light side of your values look attractive. Shoving an excel sheet in his face is not going to motivate him to budget. Men work well with examples. If you honor responsibility, point out a leader you both admire and say, "Wow he is so disciplined. It's like he is intentional with every word he says and every dollar he spends. That is so sexy."

Step three: Ask him questions. Suspend critique and ask him how he ever became so trusting with money. Without passive aggressive tones, ask how he can be so trusting with money despite not having a ton of it. You will not only learn his story, but you will get a bigger perspective about how he sees himself and his habits.

Step four: Commit to using the healthy side of your shadow every day. If your shadow is the egomaniac, commit to benefiting from her skills. For example, egomaniacs don't apologize for themselves. Notice when you apologize for yourself and commit to stopping. The more you embrace the beneficial side of your shadow's skills, the less you will judge your partner when he uses them in less beneficial ways.

Stand in your values, live your values and let your partner live in his. If his actions do have a harmful impact, like when you share a bank account, set boundaries.

Develop Your Skills

If you have ever been impatient, critical, or judgmental of your partner, it is about time you put those skills to good use. The more you use your inner judge in productive ways, the less she will lash out with unproductive words and actions. In the same way that you just explored the benefits of your partner's ego and over-spending, you are now going to find the benefits beneath your judgment.

WRITE A LETTER TO YOUR INNER JUDGE EXERCISE

Imagine that your judgment was a separate part of you. She is the highly critical, controlling and stubborn side of you that comes out when your partner pushes your buttons. See this part of you pointing and yelling at your partner, telling him what you want him to do. What does she look like? How is her body language? How does she quietly and passively judge? Write all these traits down. Get creative. If you feel your body having an adverse reaction to her, stop and breathe. Use the stress reducing EFT points depicted in the back of the book.

Common Traits of The Inner Judge:
Trusts her way is the right way.
Never doubts herself.

Has one way of doing life.

Highly opinionated.

Doesn't sway, even despite guilt tripping, anger, or peer pressure.

Can you think of moments in your life when her skills might come in handy? Have you ever stopped trusting yourself? Have you ever doubted yourself? Have you ever wished you could lay down the gauntlet and set a boundary? Well, it looks like your inner judge can help you achieve all three.

Write a letter to your inner judge, telling her when you do and don't need her skills. Most of the time, your inner judge wants to help you stand up for what you think is right, trust yourself more, and have confidence. When are these skills helpful? When are they destructive? For instance, if your partner wants to spend money on a new car, your judge can help you stand firm on your savings plan. On the other hand, if your partner is cooking dinner and you think he is doing it all wrong, your inner judge's opinion is not appropriate. Set a boundary between when you do and don't need her help.

Your inner judge's goal is not to reject and despise your partner for his imperfections. She wants to make you aware of what you've rejected, so you can make an informed choice. Will you hate your partner for his imperfections? Will you judge him for frustrating you? Will you stifle the wounds that cause each frustration? Or will you use your awareness to learn to love him and yourself more? When you feel judgmental, embrace your choices: Choose to click "Upgrade Now," get curious about what you can learn from him, and enter a new level of ease and functionality in your relationship.

Enjoy Your Saving Grace: Curiosity

What if every time you felt judgmental, you got curious? Why might he think he is right? Why do I think I'm so right? Is proving I'm right helping? What can we learn from each other? What can I learn from him? How might his way be better than my way? What skills is he using that I maybe have suppressed? Will you have to be courageously vulnerable to answer each question? Of course.

Your ego grows from being right, but your relationship grows from being curious. When your partner does that thing he does, breathe. If you assume the posture of curiosity, you will avoid another right versus wrong argument. If you need to vent, go into the bathroom and tap it out. Then practice judgment's saving grace: curiosity.

Can you get curious about how his traits can be used for good?

Can you get curious about how he is teaching you something through your Imago?

Can you get curious about the shadow he is reflecting in you?

Can you get curious about ways you can love him, and yourself, despite imperfections?

Curiosity is all about surrendering your agenda so that you can get curious about a bigger agenda, an agenda that can heal you, your partner, and your relationship.

The next time you start nitpicking your boyfriend or husband choose to upgrade.

Conditioned Response: "Why are you doing that? You should do it this way." Man, I can't believe he is so unaware. Do I have to do everything for him?

Upgraded Response: Observe what he is doing, noticing why it bothers you. If he is doing something hurtful, obviously demand that he stop. If he is just doing him, get curious about how he does life differently than you. Get curious about why you think your way is better and why he might think his way is better. Appreciate his differences instead of demanding he be just like you.

Getting curious is easier said than done. Prepare yourself for the following roadblocks.

Roadblocks On The Route To Curiosity

He will irritate you: You will judge him for how he spends money, cleans, or manages his work. You will forget you are judging him, because you will feel so justified. When this happens, get curious about how his way might be better than your way. Is he better at being trustworthy with finances while you are more controlling? Is he better at staying tidy while you are better at cleaning up? Get curious about the shadows and Imago that want to heal. Remember 90% of frustrations have to do with you, not him.

You will become impatient: You will want something that he just isn't giving you. Get curious about the learning opportunity within the moment. Is he always late? Maybe your are learning about patience. Is he indecisive? Maybe you are learning about trust. Get curious about how his patterns are reflecting deeper stories going on inside of you.

You will expect him to be perfect: Just because there is something that bothers you about your partner, doesn't mean you are supposed to leave him. No one is perfect because perfection is indefinable. If he is disorganized and you are hyper-organized, maybe you are partners for a reason. If he is very right brain and you are very left brain, maybe you are partners to create balance. Get curious about how your strengths compliment his weaknesses, and vice versa. Let your imperfections compliment each other.

A Rare Breed

If upgrading were easy, everyone would do it. Women would stop complaining about their boyfriends. Girls would stop judging their looks. Wives would never nitpick their husbands. You would never gossip about your ex-lovers. Unfortunately, most people love judgment because judgment lets them feel right. Choose to be the rare breed that would rather love than judge. This choice isn't easy, but it will heal your relationship and every relationship that touches the two of you. The truth is, upgrading out of generation-old habits is not easy, but the future generation is begging you to break through them. It is about time we journey into a new legacy together.

11

Leave a Legacy With Your Love

💜 💜 💜

"The light shines in the darkness,
and the darkness has not overcome it"
— **John** the Apostle

E very relationship is different. Some couples meet and get engaged within three months. Other people fall in love in high school and wait eight years until they get married. Other women are engaged, call it off, and move thousands of miles away to fall in love with a different kind of mission. Don't compare yourself to these people. You are not other people. You are you. Plus, you wouldn't want their relationship anyway. Their relationship will pale in comparison to yours.

Fear will tell you to compare.

Fear will tell you to take a year off to "fix" yourself.

Fear will make the clock sound like it is ticking faster than it is.

Fear will tell you that you are not complete until you find the one.

Fear will tell you many things that you are not designed to obey.

Flip back to chapter 03 and remind yourself of the purpose of fear. Fear's job is to keep you safe. Ironically, most of fear's messages are outdated and in need of an upgrade. When fear starts speaking into your relationship, feel free to speak back: "Thanks fear, but you're wrong. I don't need to compare myself for validation. I don't need to "fix" myself in order to be deserving. I don't need a man to make me feel complete. I am complete, thank you very much."

Your emotions, including fears, insecurity, and even inspiration, are sick of having one-sided conversations with you. They want you to speak up. If you don't listen to them and try to stuff them down, you will force them to speak up louder, to nag you longer, and to manifest as patterns that you will not be able to ignore.

Everyone has feelings of fear, anger, and jealousy, but not everyone has to let them destroy their relationship. Unfortunately, not everyone has the tools to navigate their feelings and the issues they create. You do! You have the tools, and its up to you to implement them. You will always have difficult feelings, but the feelings don't need to run your love life.

The truth is, emotions are, and always will be your greatest gift. You can't choose one and reject the other. You can't feel love without honoring fear. You can't feel confident without honoring jealousy. You can't feel trust without honoring doubt. If you get rid of the fear-based emotions, you have to get rid of the love based ones as well. You can't choose one without the other. You wouldn't want to make that choice. Without emotions, you would find yourself in a listless, conveyor-belt of a relationship, moving wherever logic took you.

Six years ago I was on a conveyor belt that my heart didn't want. Unfortunately, logic convinced me to stay with him: He was my best friend at that point. We had fun together. We had been together for four years. We shared all the same friends. I couldn't imagine being with anyone else, let alone watching him be with someone other than me. There was nothing "wrong" that I could point my finger to as a reason to leave. Despite logic, I broke up with him, twice. We kept getting back together out of habit or need. Each time, something deep inside me kept nagging me to wait for something better. I kept ignoring the voice. I wrote in my journal: Give me a sign! Tell me if I am supposed to stay with him or break up for good. The irony is that if I thumbed back a few pages, I would have seen dozens of signs scribbled on every single page. Pages of uncertainty, doubt, anger, hesitation. My emotions had been sending me messages for three years. I just hadn't been taught how to listen. Since I didn't listen, they got louder, until eventually I got the sign I had asked for. He cheated on me. My emotions had been trying to warn me all along, but since I didn't listen, they had to scream louder. I had been trained to suppress them. You, my love, have the tools I hadn't learned yet.

Implement what you now know. Have the courage to feel. You can't think your way into a loving relationship; you have to feel your way into one. When you do, you will break free from relationship issues that are beneath you. Finding your validation in men is beneath you. Comparing yourself to other women is beneath you. You don't deserve to be lied to, manipulated or disrespected anymore. You don't deserve that and I didn't deserve it. I was tired of struggling with the same issues over and over again. I was tired enough to figure out how to change. I hope that my journey, and the tools I've shared can help you find the change you seek. They sure helped me.

As I write this, it is my husband's birthday. As he blew out his candles I thought of a wish I made years ago. I had done the very cheesy thing of writing a list of traits I wanted in a partner. I wrote that list at the top of a waterfall, rolled it up, and threw it down. My list included: traveling together, working together, having fun, being ourselves, being able to meditate together, trustworthy, respects his parents, driven, joyful, creative, willing to hike to waterfalls like this one.

A year later, my now-husband would walk me to that same waterfall, not knowing I had imagined him a year prior. A year after that, he would travel with me to India, where we would work together to help victims of sexual abuse. A year after that, we would travel to Vietnam, where we would hike ten miles through a jungle and zip line to a tree house where he would propose. I said yes, and I was able to say yes because I had said yes to upgrading the issues and fears that had no place in a healthy relationship.

Now, it is your turn.

My Hope For You

Your relationship status shouldn't be your biggest source of stress, but the place you go to de-stress. I have seen women move from frustrating relationships to freeing relationships, and you deserve the same.

I wrote *I Can't Believe I Dated Him* so you can rebel against relationship cycles that are beneath you. I want to talk to you, and tell you how deserving you are of everything you ever wanted in a relationship. You deserve joy, and trust and respect and depth. I want to explore your patterns and show you how your current issues are opportunities to step into your strengths. I want to journey with you as you embrace each opportunity, so you can leave a legacy with your love.

A Woman Who U.P.G.R.A.D.E.S

Doesn't let past relationships define her future

Doesn't need a year off to know she is deserving or worthy of love

Trusts herself and her decisions

Respects herself enough to break up with the wrong partners

Never settles, but enjoys dating

Acts on her highest intentions despite doubt and fear

Enjoys weddings and means it when she says congratulations

Is too busy empowering herself and her friends to disempower her partner

Knows who she is, what she wants, and isn't afraid to ask for it

Share Your Shifts

I love to hear about love. I truly believe that the purpose of life is to learn to love well, whether that means staying single, getting married, or practicing a combination of both. When I see clients loving themselves and their partners well, I feel alive. To share your emotional and relationship transformations, email me at jackie@theupgradedwoman.com

Inevitably, when you change how you approach relationships, you change how you approach every aspect of life. Life is a relationship. Feel free to share successes you have in your business, your health, and your personal life as well.

If you enjoy consistent reminders to love mindfully, you will like my weekly blog. I address topics like betrayal, trust, and heartbreak that arise in personal and professional relationships. You can subscribe by clicking the "Free Gift Included" button on the top of my website: www.TheUpgradedWoman.com

No matter how dark your situation may seem, you are light; where the light goes, darkness cannot last.

The Healthy & Unhealthy Sides Of Your Emotions

Your emotions have healthy and unhealthy sides. It is your choice how you will use them. Use the summaries below as you journey into the healthiest expression of you.

FEAR

The protector | anxious vs. detail oriented | seeks safety | when threatened assumes the worst | dark side feels better by taking control | light side feels better by getting creative about courses of action | loves taking action to prove fear's wrong

UNCERTAINTY

The perfectionist | worry vs. surrender | seeks control | when threatened makes spontaneous decisions | dark side feels better by getting answers | light side feels better by surrendering control | loves hoping in best case scenarios

DOUBT

The spiritual | pessimistic vs. realistic | seeks answers | when threatened stifles excitement | dark side feels better by lowering expectations and seeking tangible evidence | light side feels better by trusting in higher power | loves high expectations and taking faith-filled risk

EMPATHY

The coach & friend | optimistic vs. coddling | when threatened excuses bad behavior or takes the blame | dark side feels better by fixing | light side feels better by respecting | loves allowing independence

SHAME

The grounded | apologetic vs. free | seeks approval | when threatened self-edits | dark side feels better by downplaying excitement | light side feels better by rebelling against lies | loves making choices independent from the past

INSECURITY

The emotionally sensitive | people pleasing vs. compassionate | seeks success | when threatened- hides and seeks solitude | dark side feels better by comparing yourself to others | light side feels better by being honest and vulnerable | loves creating home and familiarity

ANGER

The activist | passionate vs. explosive | seeks rights | when threatened makes rash decisions | dark side feels better by justifying and fighting against something | light side feels better by fighting for someone | loves seeking justice

JUDGMENT

The intellectual | stubborn vs. self-aware | seeks reason | when threatened tries to prove you're right and they're wrong | dark side feels better by proving yourself | light side feels better by getting curious or appreciating partner's differences | loves seeking oneness instead of hierarchy.

Emotional Freedom Technique
Tapping Chart

Lightly tap each point 7-10 times while repeating a reminder phrase for your problem.

Acknowledgments

God, thank you for making us layered and emotional, even when it is uncomfortable. You have an odd sense of humor and an irrational trust in how we use our free will.

Jake, thank you for loving me, and for staying rooted as I spiral down every emotion laid out in this book.

Mom, thank you from the deep places, for believing in the unseen, and for showing me how to see it.

Dad, I don't know how I would have finished this book in four weeks if it wasn't for your work ethic and determination in my blood. Sharon, I am forever grateful that my dad found you. We are lucky to have you in the family.

Lauren, wow. Thanks for everything.

Gram and Grandpa, keep sharing your medal-worthy stories. You're my inspiration. I felt you encouraging me before I was even born.

Queen Bun, thank you for never apologizing for the royal powerhouse you are. You're 100 years worth of inspiration, literally.

Joe and Shelly, Megan and Jason, it is not too common a girl inherits a family as amazing as you. Your texts and prayers kept me going.

Thank you to my sheep pack: Audrey, Amy, Arlene, Ariya, Bentley, Danielle, Kathryn, Kristen, Kristina, and Oti. You are all a bunch of old wise women in jaw-dropping human suits, and I couldn't be more proud to call you friends.

DB, soul mate, thanks for introducing me to the one true love, and my one true love. You wear courage and love very well.

Katy, you trusted me with the hours you spent as my guinea pig. Let's revisit those days soon. Jen, you are the best cheerleader, friend, traveler, and world changer. I heard your encouraging voice many times during the writing process. Alexia, thanks for teaching me what "passive" really means.

Every mentor who's influenced me, I hope I'm passing on your wisdom wisely: Dawson Church, Dale Teplitz, Margaret Lynch, Alina Frank, Bethany Long and Sherrie Rice Smith, you all have a unique gift at making complex ideas captivating.

Where would this book be without Angela and the entire Difference Press team? It would still be in my head. Cynthia, you are a saint for dealing with my crazy mind.

The MJ Publishing Team, thank you for the time, the grace and the belief in me. I'm so excited to continue this journey.

Lastly, and most humbly, I want to thank every client who has ever had the courage to show me their whole heart. I am forever grateful for you and forever honored to have the privilege to hold your stories.

About The Author

Jackie Viramontez is a relationship coach and best-selling author. She empowers women to pursue their ideal relationship in private and group sessions. Certified in Emotional Freedom Techniques, Jackie specializes in redefining the role fear, perfectionism, and people pleasing play in a woman's life.

The daughter of a holistic healthcare practitioner, she started meditating at six and using mindfulness at ten. After receiving a degree in Journalism from Syracuse University, Semester at Sea and Teach for America, she decided the best way to empower women was through tailored coaching.

She has taught alongside Dawson Church and Dale Teplitz, and hosted workshops with women's organizations nationally and internationally.

An advocate for women's rights, she has traveled to India, China, and the far corners of Southern California, to create and teach curriculums that heal the side effects of relationship trauma and sexual abuse.

In her free time, she downloads podcasts, cooks green things, and explores Los Angeles with her filmmaker husband, Jake.

Thank You

Thank you for reading and seeking answers to the questions in your heart. To help you put the new insights into practice, I've created a free toolkit you can easily access online. Download now by following the link www.TheUpgradedWoman.com. Put your name and email in the form fields, and click Download Toolkit. After you confirm your email address, you will be able to access cheat sheets and video resources that support your transformation.

The Upgraded Woman Toolkit includes:

THE QUIZ: Discover which fear-based emotion is causing your relationship frustration.

FREE CHEAT SHEETS: Use simple reference guides to navigate messy emotions.

FREE VIDEO SERIES: Master the seven habits that leave a legacy with your love. I will walk you through the core concepts in the book in a short video format.

FREE STRATEGY SESSION: Set the reset button on your relationship story in a complimentary 30 min phone call. This is not a call for those who want to stay surface level. We will go deep, find the roots, and end with a plan to experience the love you deserve. You can apply for a strategy session by choosing a date/time and completing the application questions here: https://theupgradedwoman. acuityscheduling.com/

You deserve the peace and possibility that comes from an empowering love story. If you are holding this book, you have already made your relationship a priority, and I am here to journey with you.

Share your success story here:
Email: jackie@theupgradedwoman.com
Phone: (424)-272-1693

I am looking forward to hearing your story.
Live love,
Jackie Viramontez

A free eBook edition is available with the purchase of this book.

To claim your free eBook edition:

1. Download the Shelfie app.
2. Write your name in upper case in the box.
3. Use the Shelfie app to submit a photo.
4. Download your eBook to any device.

Shelfie

A free eBook edition is available
with the purchase of this print book.

CLEARLY PRINT YOUR NAME ABOVE IN UPPER CASE

Instructions to claim your free eBook edition:
1. Download the Shelfie app for Android or iOS
2. Write your name in **UPPER CASE** above
3. Use the Shelfie app to submit a photo
4. Download your eBook to any device

Print & Digital Together Forever.

Snap a photo   Free eBook   Read anywhere

Morgan James makes all of our titles available
through the Library for All Charity Organizations.

www.LibraryForAll.org

CPSIA information can be obtained
at www.ICGtesting.com
Printed in the USA
LVOW10*1030060817
544018LV00009B/72/P